ADHD *Planner*

INFORMATION

NAME

ADDRESS

E-MAIL ADDRESS

WEBSITE

PHONE   **FAX**

EMERGENCY CONTACT PERSON

PHONE   **FAX**

DAY GOALS

1 ....
2 ....
3 ....

DATE
WEEK
LOCATION
WEIGHT

Mood Tracker 😟 😐 😖 😢 😠 😃

BEHAVIOR

INATTENTION

SHORT ATTENTION	① ② ③ ④ ⑤ ⑥ ⑦ ⑧ ⑨ ⑩
UNMOTIVATED / BORED	① ② ③ ④ ⑤ ⑥ ⑦ ⑧ ⑨ ⑩
SHORT ATTENTION	① ② ③ ④ ⑤ ⑥ ⑦ ⑧ ⑨ ⑩
FORGETFUL / CONFUSIONED	① ② ③ ④ ⑤ ⑥ ⑦ ⑧ ⑨ ⑩

HYPERACTIVITY

CONSTANTLY MOVING / TALKING	① ② ③ ④ ⑤ ⑥ ⑦ ⑧ ⑨ ⑩
STRUGGLING TO SIT STILL	① ② ③ ④ ⑤ ⑥ ⑦ ⑧ ⑨ ⑩
TOUCHING THINGS REPEATEDLY	① ② ③ ④ ⑤ ⑥ ⑦ ⑧ ⑨ ⑩
DIFFICULT SLEEPING	① ② ③ ④ ⑤ ⑥ ⑦ ⑧ ⑨ ⑩

IMPULSIVITY

ACTING WITHOUT THINKING	① ② ③ ④ ⑤ ⑥ ⑦ ⑧ ⑨ ⑩
INTERRUPTING OTHERS	① ② ③ ④ ⑤ ⑥ ⑦ ⑧ ⑨ ⑩
EASILY FRUSTRATED	① ② ③ ④ ⑤ ⑥ ⑦ ⑧ ⑨ ⑩
UNABLE TO HOLD BACK EMOTIONS	① ② ③ ④ ⑤ ⑥ ⑦ ⑧ ⑨ ⑩

MEALS

MEDICATIONS

Water Tracker 🍼 🍼 🍼 🍼 🍼 🍼 🍼

NOTES

....
....

DAY GOALS	
1	DATE
2	WEEK
3	LOCATION
	WEIGHT

Mood Tracker 😟 😐 😖 😢 😠 😃

BEHAVIOR

INATTENTION

SHORT ATTENTION	① ② ③ ④ ⑤ ⑥ ⑦ ⑧ ⑨ ⑩
UNMOTIVATED / BORED	① ② ③ ④ ⑤ ⑥ ⑦ ⑧ ⑨ ⑩
SHORT ATTENTION	① ② ③ ④ ⑤ ⑥ ⑦ ⑧ ⑨ ⑩
FORGETFUL / CONFUSIONED	① ② ③ ④ ⑤ ⑥ ⑦ ⑧ ⑨ ⑩

HYPERACTIVITY

CONSTANTLY MOVING / TALKING	① ② ③ ④ ⑤ ⑥ ⑦ ⑧ ⑨ ⑩
STRUGGLING TO SIT STILL	① ② ③ ④ ⑤ ⑥ ⑦ ⑧ ⑨ ⑩
TOUCHING THINGS REPEATEDLY	① ② ③ ④ ⑤ ⑥ ⑦ ⑧ ⑨ ⑩
DIFFICULT SLEEPING	① ② ③ ④ ⑤ ⑥ ⑦ ⑧ ⑨ ⑩

IMPULSIVITY

ACTING WITHOUT THINKING	① ② ③ ④ ⑤ ⑥ ⑦ ⑧ ⑨ ⑩
INTERRUPTING OTHERS	① ② ③ ④ ⑤ ⑥ ⑦ ⑧ ⑨ ⑩
EASILY FRUSTRATED	① ② ③ ④ ⑤ ⑥ ⑦ ⑧ ⑨ ⑩
UNABLE TO HOLD BACK EMOTIONS	① ② ③ ④ ⑤ ⑥ ⑦ ⑧ ⑨ ⑩

MEALS	MEDICATIONS

Water Tracker 🍼 🍼 🍼 🍼 🍼 🍼 🍼

NOTES

....
....

DAY GOALS

1 ....
2 ....
3 ....

DATE
WEEK
LOCATION
WEIGHT

Mood Tracker ☹ 😐 😖 🙁 😠 😀

BEHAVIOR

INATTENTION

SHORT ATTENTION	① ② ③ ④ ⑤ ⑥ ⑦ ⑧ ⑨ ⑩
UNMOTIVATED / BORED	① ② ③ ④ ⑤ ⑥ ⑦ ⑧ ⑨ ⑩
SHORT ATTENTION	① ② ③ ④ ⑤ ⑥ ⑦ ⑧ ⑨ ⑩
FORGETFUL / CONFUSIONED	① ② ③ ④ ⑤ ⑥ ⑦ ⑧ ⑨ ⑩

HYPERACTIVITY

CONSTANTLY MOVING / TALKING	① ② ③ ④ ⑤ ⑥ ⑦ ⑧ ⑨ ⑩
STRUGGLING TO SIT STILL	① ② ③ ④ ⑤ ⑥ ⑦ ⑧ ⑨ ⑩
TOUCHING THINGS REPEATEDLY	① ② ③ ④ ⑤ ⑥ ⑦ ⑧ ⑨ ⑩
DIFFICULT SLEEPING	① ② ③ ④ ⑤ ⑥ ⑦ ⑧ ⑨ ⑩

IMPULSIVITY

ACTING WITHOUT THINKING	① ② ③ ④ ⑤ ⑥ ⑦ ⑧ ⑨ ⑩
INTERRUPTING OTHERS	① ② ③ ④ ⑤ ⑥ ⑦ ⑧ ⑨ ⑩
EASILY FRUSTRATED	① ② ③ ④ ⑤ ⑥ ⑦ ⑧ ⑨ ⑩
UNABLE TO HOLD BACK EMOTIONS	① ② ③ ④ ⑤ ⑥ ⑦ ⑧ ⑨ ⑩

MEALS

MEDICATIONS

Water Tracker 🍼 🍼 🍼 🍼 🍼 🍼 🍼

NOTES

....
....

DAY GOALS

1 ....
2 ....
3 ....

DATE
WEEK
LOCATION
WEIGHT

Mood Tracker ☹ 😐 😖 😢 😠 😃

BEHAVIOR

INATTENTION

SHORT ATTENTION	① ② ③ ④ ⑤ ⑥ ⑦ ⑧ ⑨ ⑩
UNMOTIVATED / BORED	① ② ③ ④ ⑤ ⑥ ⑦ ⑧ ⑨ ⑩
SHORT ATTENTION	① ② ③ ④ ⑤ ⑥ ⑦ ⑧ ⑨ ⑩
FORGETFUL / CONFUSIONED	① ② ③ ④ ⑤ ⑥ ⑦ ⑧ ⑨ ⑩

HYPERACTIVITY

CONSTANTLY MOVING / TALKING	① ② ③ ④ ⑤ ⑥ ⑦ ⑧ ⑨ ⑩
STRUGGLING TO SIT STILL	① ② ③ ④ ⑤ ⑥ ⑦ ⑧ ⑨ ⑩
TOUCHING THINGS REPEATEDLY	① ② ③ ④ ⑤ ⑥ ⑦ ⑧ ⑨ ⑩
DIFFICULT SLEEPING	① ② ③ ④ ⑤ ⑥ ⑦ ⑧ ⑨ ⑩

IMPULSIVITY

ACTING WITHOUT THINKING	① ② ③ ④ ⑤ ⑥ ⑦ ⑧ ⑨ ⑩
INTERRUPTING OTHERS	① ② ③ ④ ⑤ ⑥ ⑦ ⑧ ⑨ ⑩
EASILY FRUSTRATED	① ② ③ ④ ⑤ ⑥ ⑦ ⑧ ⑨ ⑩
UNABLE TO HOLD BACK EMOTIONS	① ② ③ ④ ⑤ ⑥ ⑦ ⑧ ⑨ ⑩

MEALS

MEDICATIONS

Water Tracker 🍶 🍶 🍶 🍶 🍶 🍶 🍶

NOTES

....
....

DAY GOALS

1 ....
2 ....
3 ....

DATE
WEEK
LOCATION
WEIGHT

Mood Tracker ☹ 😐 😖 😢 😠 😃

BEHAVIOR

INATTENTION

Behavior	Rating
SHORT ATTENTION	① ② ③ ④ ⑤ ⑥ ⑦ ⑧ ⑨ ⑩
UNMOTIVATED / BORED	① ② ③ ④ ⑤ ⑥ ⑦ ⑧ ⑨ ⑩
SHORT ATTENTION	① ② ③ ④ ⑤ ⑥ ⑦ ⑧ ⑨ ⑩
FORGETFUL / CONFUSIONED	① ② ③ ④ ⑤ ⑥ ⑦ ⑧ ⑨ ⑩

HYPERACTIVITY

Behavior	Rating
CONSTANTLY MOVING / TALKING	① ② ③ ④ ⑤ ⑥ ⑦ ⑧ ⑨ ⑩
STRUGGLING TO SIT STILL	① ② ③ ④ ⑤ ⑥ ⑦ ⑧ ⑨ ⑩
TOUCHING THINGS REPEATEDLY	① ② ③ ④ ⑤ ⑥ ⑦ ⑧ ⑨ ⑩
DIFFICULT SLEEPING	① ② ③ ④ ⑤ ⑥ ⑦ ⑧ ⑨ ⑩

IMPULSIVITY

Behavior	Rating
ACTING WITHOUT THINKING	① ② ③ ④ ⑤ ⑥ ⑦ ⑧ ⑨ ⑩
INTERRUPTING OTHERS	① ② ③ ④ ⑤ ⑥ ⑦ ⑧ ⑨ ⑩
EASILY FRUSTRATED	① ② ③ ④ ⑤ ⑥ ⑦ ⑧ ⑨ ⑩
UNABLE TO HOLD BACK EMOTIONS	① ② ③ ④ ⑤ ⑥ ⑦ ⑧ ⑨ ⑩

MEALS

MEDICATIONS

Water Tracker 🍼 🍼 🍼 🍼 🍼 🍼 🍼

NOTES

....
....

DAY GOALS		DATE
1		WEEK
2		LOCATION
3		WEIGHT

Mood Tracker 😟 😐 😖 😢 😠 😃

BEHAVIOR

INATTENTION

SHORT ATTENTION	① ② ③ ④ ⑤ ⑥ ⑦ ⑧ ⑨ ⑩
UNMOTIVATED / BORED	① ② ③ ④ ⑤ ⑥ ⑦ ⑧ ⑨ ⑩
SHORT ATTENTION	① ② ③ ④ ⑤ ⑥ ⑦ ⑧ ⑨ ⑩
FORGETFUL / CONFUSIONED	① ② ③ ④ ⑤ ⑥ ⑦ ⑧ ⑨ ⑩

HYPERACTIVITY

CONSTANTLY MOVING / TALKING	① ② ③ ④ ⑤ ⑥ ⑦ ⑧ ⑨ ⑩
STRUGGLING TO SIT STILL	① ② ③ ④ ⑤ ⑥ ⑦ ⑧ ⑨ ⑩
TOUCHING THINGS REPEATEDLY	① ② ③ ④ ⑤ ⑥ ⑦ ⑧ ⑨ ⑩
DIFFICULT SLEEPING	① ② ③ ④ ⑤ ⑥ ⑦ ⑧ ⑨ ⑩

IMPULSIVITY

ACTING WITHOUT THINKING	① ② ③ ④ ⑤ ⑥ ⑦ ⑧ ⑨ ⑩
INTERRUPTING OTHERS	① ② ③ ④ ⑤ ⑥ ⑦ ⑧ ⑨ ⑩
EASILY FRUSTRATED	① ② ③ ④ ⑤ ⑥ ⑦ ⑧ ⑨ ⑩
UNABLE TO HOLD BACK EMOTIONS	① ② ③ ④ ⑤ ⑥ ⑦ ⑧ ⑨ ⑩

MEALS	MEDICATIONS

Water Tracker 🍼 🍼 🍼 🍼 🍼 🍼 🍼

NOTES

....
....

DAY GOALS

1 ....
2 ....
3 ....

DATE
WEEK
LOCATION
WEIGHT

Mood Tracker

BEHAVIOR

INATTENTION

SHORT ATTENTION	① ② ③ ④ ⑤ ⑥ ⑦ ⑧ ⑨ ⑩
UNMOTIVATED / BORED	① ② ③ ④ ⑤ ⑥ ⑦ ⑧ ⑨ ⑩
SHORT ATTENTION	① ② ③ ④ ⑤ ⑥ ⑦ ⑧ ⑨ ⑩
FORGETFUL / CONFUSIONED	① ② ③ ④ ⑤ ⑥ ⑦ ⑧ ⑨ ⑩

HYPERACTIVITY

CONSTANTLY MOVING / TALKING	① ② ③ ④ ⑤ ⑥ ⑦ ⑧ ⑨ ⑩
STRUGGLING TO SIT STILL	① ② ③ ④ ⑤ ⑥ ⑦ ⑧ ⑨ ⑩
TOUCHING THINGS REPEATEDLY	① ② ③ ④ ⑤ ⑥ ⑦ ⑧ ⑨ ⑩
DIFFICULT SLEEPING	① ② ③ ④ ⑤ ⑥ ⑦ ⑧ ⑨ ⑩

IMPULSIVITY

ACTING WITHOUT THINKING	① ② ③ ④ ⑤ ⑥ ⑦ ⑧ ⑨ ⑩
INTERRUPTING OTHERS	① ② ③ ④ ⑤ ⑥ ⑦ ⑧ ⑨ ⑩
EASILY FRUSTRATED	① ② ③ ④ ⑤ ⑥ ⑦ ⑧ ⑨ ⑩
UNABLE TO HOLD BACK EMOTIONS	① ② ③ ④ ⑤ ⑥ ⑦ ⑧ ⑨ ⑩

MEALS

MEDICATIONS

Water Tracker

NOTES

....
....

DAY GOALS	
1	DATE
2	WEEK
3	LOCATION
	WEIGHT

Mood Tracker 😟 😐 😖 😢 😠 😀

BEHAVIOR

INATTENTION

SHORT ATTENTION	① ② ③ ④ ⑤ ⑥ ⑦ ⑧ ⑨ ⑩
UNMOTIVATED / BORED	① ② ③ ④ ⑤ ⑥ ⑦ ⑧ ⑨ ⑩
SHORT ATTENTION	① ② ③ ④ ⑤ ⑥ ⑦ ⑧ ⑨ ⑩
FORGETFUL / CONFUSIONED	① ② ③ ④ ⑤ ⑥ ⑦ ⑧ ⑨ ⑩

HYPERACTIVITY

CONSTANTLY MOVING / TALKING	① ② ③ ④ ⑤ ⑥ ⑦ ⑧ ⑨ ⑩
STRUGGLING TO SIT STILL	① ② ③ ④ ⑤ ⑥ ⑦ ⑧ ⑨ ⑩
TOUCHING THINGS REPEATEDLY	① ② ③ ④ ⑤ ⑥ ⑦ ⑧ ⑨ ⑩
DIFFICULT SLEEPING	① ② ③ ④ ⑤ ⑥ ⑦ ⑧ ⑨ ⑩

IMPULSIVITY

ACTING WITHOUT THINKING	① ② ③ ④ ⑤ ⑥ ⑦ ⑧ ⑨ ⑩
INTERRUPTING OTHERS	① ② ③ ④ ⑤ ⑥ ⑦ ⑧ ⑨ ⑩
EASILY FRUSTRATED	① ② ③ ④ ⑤ ⑥ ⑦ ⑧ ⑨ ⑩
UNABLE TO HOLD BACK EMOTIONS	① ② ③ ④ ⑤ ⑥ ⑦ ⑧ ⑨ ⑩

MEALS	MEDICATIONS

Water Tracker 🍼 🍼 🍼 🍼 🍼 🍼 🍼

NOTES

....
....

DAY GOALS	
1	
2	
3	

DATE
WEEK
LOCATION
WEIGHT

Mood Tracker 😕 😐 😣 🥲 😠 😃

BEHAVIOR

INATTENTION

SHORT ATTENTION	① ② ③ ④ ⑤ ⑥ ⑦ ⑧ ⑨ ⑩
UNMOTIVATED / BORED	① ② ③ ④ ⑤ ⑥ ⑦ ⑧ ⑨ ⑩
SHORT ATTENTION	① ② ③ ④ ⑤ ⑥ ⑦ ⑧ ⑨ ⑩
FORGETFUL / CONFUSIONED	① ② ③ ④ ⑤ ⑥ ⑦ ⑧ ⑨ ⑩

HYPERACTIVITY

CONSTANTLY MOVING / TALKING	① ② ③ ④ ⑤ ⑥ ⑦ ⑧ ⑨ ⑩
STRUGGLING TO SIT STILL	① ② ③ ④ ⑤ ⑥ ⑦ ⑧ ⑨ ⑩
TOUCHING THINGS REPEATEDLY	① ② ③ ④ ⑤ ⑥ ⑦ ⑧ ⑨ ⑩
DIFFICULT SLEEPING	① ② ③ ④ ⑤ ⑥ ⑦ ⑧ ⑨ ⑩

IMPULSIVITY

ACTING WITHOUT THINKING	① ② ③ ④ ⑤ ⑥ ⑦ ⑧ ⑨ ⑩
INTERRUPTING OTHERS	① ② ③ ④ ⑤ ⑥ ⑦ ⑧ ⑨ ⑩
EASILY FRUSTRATED	① ② ③ ④ ⑤ ⑥ ⑦ ⑧ ⑨ ⑩
UNABLE TO HOLD BACK EMOTIONS	① ② ③ ④ ⑤ ⑥ ⑦ ⑧ ⑨ ⑩

MEALS	MEDICATIONS

Water Tracker 🍼 🍼 🍼 🍼 🍼 🍼 🍼

NOTES

....
....

DAY GOALS	
1	DATE
2	WEEK
3	LOCATION
	WEIGHT

Mood Tracker

BEHAVIOR

INATTENTION

SHORT ATTENTION	① ② ③ ④ ⑤ ⑥ ⑦ ⑧ ⑨ ⑩
UNMOTIVATED / BORED	① ② ③ ④ ⑤ ⑥ ⑦ ⑧ ⑨ ⑩
SHORT ATTENTION	① ② ③ ④ ⑤ ⑥ ⑦ ⑧ ⑨ ⑩
FORGETFUL / CONFUSIONED	① ② ③ ④ ⑤ ⑥ ⑦ ⑧ ⑨ ⑩

HYPERACTIVITY

CONSTANTLY MOVING / TALKING	① ② ③ ④ ⑤ ⑥ ⑦ ⑧ ⑨ ⑩
STRUGGLING TO SIT STILL	① ② ③ ④ ⑤ ⑥ ⑦ ⑧ ⑨ ⑩
TOUCHING THINGS REPEATEDLY	① ② ③ ④ ⑤ ⑥ ⑦ ⑧ ⑨ ⑩
DIFFICULT SLEEPING	① ② ③ ④ ⑤ ⑥ ⑦ ⑧ ⑨ ⑩

IMPULSIVITY

ACTING WITHOUT THINKING	① ② ③ ④ ⑤ ⑥ ⑦ ⑧ ⑨ ⑩
INTERRUPTING OTHERS	① ② ③ ④ ⑤ ⑥ ⑦ ⑧ ⑨ ⑩
EASILY FRUSTRATED	① ② ③ ④ ⑤ ⑥ ⑦ ⑧ ⑨ ⑩
UNABLE TO HOLD BACK EMOTIONS	① ② ③ ④ ⑤ ⑥ ⑦ ⑧ ⑨ ⑩

MEALS	MEDICATIONS

Water Tracker

NOTES

....
....

DAY GOALS

1 ....
2 ....
3 ....

DATE
WEEK
LOCATION
WEIGHT

Mood Tracker ☹️ 😐 😖 🥲 😠 😃

BEHAVIOR

INATTENTION

SHORT ATTENTION	① ② ③ ④ ⑤ ⑥ ⑦ ⑧ ⑨ ⑩
UNMOTIVATED / BORED	① ② ③ ④ ⑤ ⑥ ⑦ ⑧ ⑨ ⑩
SHORT ATTENTION	① ② ③ ④ ⑤ ⑥ ⑦ ⑧ ⑨ ⑩
FORGETFUL / CONFUSIONED	① ② ③ ④ ⑤ ⑥ ⑦ ⑧ ⑨ ⑩

HYPERACTIVITY

CONSTANTLY MOVING / TALKING	① ② ③ ④ ⑤ ⑥ ⑦ ⑧ ⑨ ⑩
STRUGGLING TO SIT STILL	① ② ③ ④ ⑤ ⑥ ⑦ ⑧ ⑨ ⑩
TOUCHING THINGS REPEATEDLY	① ② ③ ④ ⑤ ⑥ ⑦ ⑧ ⑨ ⑩
DIFFICULT SLEEPING	① ② ③ ④ ⑤ ⑥ ⑦ ⑧ ⑨ ⑩

IMPULSIVITY

ACTING WITHOUT THINKING	① ② ③ ④ ⑤ ⑥ ⑦ ⑧ ⑨ ⑩
INTERRUPTING OTHERS	① ② ③ ④ ⑤ ⑥ ⑦ ⑧ ⑨ ⑩
EASILY FRUSTRATED	① ② ③ ④ ⑤ ⑥ ⑦ ⑧ ⑨ ⑩
UNABLE TO HOLD BACK EMOTIONS	① ② ③ ④ ⑤ ⑥ ⑦ ⑧ ⑨ ⑩

MEALS	MEDICATIONS

Water Tracker 🍼 🍼 🍼 🍼 🍼 🍼 🍼

NOTES

....
....

DAY GOALS	
1	DATE
2	WEEK
3	LOCATION
	WEIGHT

Mood Tracker 😞 😐 😖 😢 😠 😃

BEHAVIOR

INATTENTION

SHORT ATTENTION	① ② ③ ④ ⑤ ⑥ ⑦ ⑧ ⑨ ⑩
UNMOTIVATED / BORED	① ② ③ ④ ⑤ ⑥ ⑦ ⑧ ⑨ ⑩
SHORT ATTENTION	① ② ③ ④ ⑤ ⑥ ⑦ ⑧ ⑨ ⑩
FORGETFUL / CONFUSIONED	① ② ③ ④ ⑤ ⑥ ⑦ ⑧ ⑨ ⑩

HYPERACTIVITY

CONSTANTLY MOVING / TALKING	① ② ③ ④ ⑤ ⑥ ⑦ ⑧ ⑨ ⑩
STRUGGLING TO SIT STILL	① ② ③ ④ ⑤ ⑥ ⑦ ⑧ ⑨ ⑩
TOUCHING THINGS REPEATEDLY	① ② ③ ④ ⑤ ⑥ ⑦ ⑧ ⑨ ⑩
DIFFICULT SLEEPING	① ② ③ ④ ⑤ ⑥ ⑦ ⑧ ⑨ ⑩

IMPULSIVITY

ACTING WITHOUT THINKING	① ② ③ ④ ⑤ ⑥ ⑦ ⑧ ⑨ ⑩
INTERRUPTING OTHERS	① ② ③ ④ ⑤ ⑥ ⑦ ⑧ ⑨ ⑩
EASILY FRUSTRATED	① ② ③ ④ ⑤ ⑥ ⑦ ⑧ ⑨ ⑩
UNABLE TO HOLD BACK EMOTIONS	① ② ③ ④ ⑤ ⑥ ⑦ ⑧ ⑨ ⑩

MEALS	MEDICATIONS

Water Tracker 🍼 🍼 🍼 🍼 🍼 🍼 🍼

NOTES

....
....

DAY GOALS	
1	
2	
3	

DATE
WEEK
LOCATION
WEIGHT

Mood Tracker 😟 😐 😖 😢 😠 😃

BEHAVIOR

INATTENTION

SHORT ATTENTION	① ② ③ ④ ⑤ ⑥ ⑦ ⑧ ⑨ ⑩
UNMOTIVATED / BORED	① ② ③ ④ ⑤ ⑥ ⑦ ⑧ ⑨ ⑩
SHORT ATTENTION	① ② ③ ④ ⑤ ⑥ ⑦ ⑧ ⑨ ⑩
FORGETFUL / CONFUSIONED	① ② ③ ④ ⑤ ⑥ ⑦ ⑧ ⑨ ⑩

HYPERACTIVITY

CONSTANTLY MOVING / TALKING	① ② ③ ④ ⑤ ⑥ ⑦ ⑧ ⑨ ⑩
STRUGGLING TO SIT STILL	① ② ③ ④ ⑤ ⑥ ⑦ ⑧ ⑨ ⑩
TOUCHING THINGS REPEATEDLY	① ② ③ ④ ⑤ ⑥ ⑦ ⑧ ⑨ ⑩
DIFFICULT SLEEPING	① ② ③ ④ ⑤ ⑥ ⑦ ⑧ ⑨ ⑩

IMPULSIVITY

ACTING WITHOUT THINKING	① ② ③ ④ ⑤ ⑥ ⑦ ⑧ ⑨ ⑩
INTERRUPTING OTHERS	① ② ③ ④ ⑤ ⑥ ⑦ ⑧ ⑨ ⑩
EASILY FRUSTRATED	① ② ③ ④ ⑤ ⑥ ⑦ ⑧ ⑨ ⑩
UNABLE TO HOLD BACK EMOTIONS	① ② ③ ④ ⑤ ⑥ ⑦ ⑧ ⑨ ⑩

MEALS	MEDICATIONS

Water Tracker 🍼 🍼 🍼 🍼 🍼 🍼 🍼

NOTES

....
....

DAY GOALS

1 ....
2 ....
3 ....

DATE
WEEK
LOCATION
WEIGHT

Mood Tracker 😟 😐 😖 😢 😠 😃

BEHAVIOR

INATTENTION

SHORT ATTENTION	① ② ③ ④ ⑤ ⑥ ⑦ ⑧ ⑨ ⑩
UNMOTIVATED / BORED	① ② ③ ④ ⑤ ⑥ ⑦ ⑧ ⑨ ⑩
SHORT ATTENTION	① ② ③ ④ ⑤ ⑥ ⑦ ⑧ ⑨ ⑩
FORGETFUL / CONFUSIONED	① ② ③ ④ ⑤ ⑥ ⑦ ⑧ ⑨ ⑩

HYPERACTIVITY

CONSTANTLY MOVING / TALKING	① ② ③ ④ ⑤ ⑥ ⑦ ⑧ ⑨ ⑩
STRUGGLING TO SIT STILL	① ② ③ ④ ⑤ ⑥ ⑦ ⑧ ⑨ ⑩
TOUCHING THINGS REPEATEDLY	① ② ③ ④ ⑤ ⑥ ⑦ ⑧ ⑨ ⑩
DIFFICULT SLEEPING	① ② ③ ④ ⑤ ⑥ ⑦ ⑧ ⑨ ⑩

IMPULSIVITY

ACTING WITHOUT THINKING	① ② ③ ④ ⑤ ⑥ ⑦ ⑧ ⑨ ⑩
INTERRUPTING OTHERS	① ② ③ ④ ⑤ ⑥ ⑦ ⑧ ⑨ ⑩
EASILY FRUSTRATED	① ② ③ ④ ⑤ ⑥ ⑦ ⑧ ⑨ ⑩
UNABLE TO HOLD BACK EMOTIONS	① ② ③ ④ ⑤ ⑥ ⑦ ⑧ ⑨ ⑩

MEALS

MEDICATIONS

Water Tracker 🍼 🍼 🍼 🍼 🍼 🍼 🍼

NOTES

....
....

DAY GOALS

1 ....
2 ....
3 ....

DATE
WEEK
LOCATION
WEIGHT

Mood Tracker ☹ 😐 😖 😢 😠 😃

BEHAVIOR

INATTENTION

Behavior	Rating
SHORT ATTENTION	① ② ③ ④ ⑤ ⑥ ⑦ ⑧ ⑨ ⑩
UNMOTIVATED / BORED	① ② ③ ④ ⑤ ⑥ ⑦ ⑧ ⑨ ⑩
SHORT ATTENTION	① ② ③ ④ ⑤ ⑥ ⑦ ⑧ ⑨ ⑩
FORGETFUL / CONFUSIONED	① ② ③ ④ ⑤ ⑥ ⑦ ⑧ ⑨ ⑩

HYPERACTIVITY

Behavior	Rating
CONSTANTLY MOVING / TALKING	① ② ③ ④ ⑤ ⑥ ⑦ ⑧ ⑨ ⑩
STRUGGLING TO SIT STILL	① ② ③ ④ ⑤ ⑥ ⑦ ⑧ ⑨ ⑩
TOUCHING THINGS REPEATEDLY	① ② ③ ④ ⑤ ⑥ ⑦ ⑧ ⑨ ⑩
DIFFICULT SLEEPING	① ② ③ ④ ⑤ ⑥ ⑦ ⑧ ⑨ ⑩

IMPULSIVITY

Behavior	Rating
ACTING WITHOUT THINKING	① ② ③ ④ ⑤ ⑥ ⑦ ⑧ ⑨ ⑩
INTERRUPTING OTHERS	① ② ③ ④ ⑤ ⑥ ⑦ ⑧ ⑨ ⑩
EASILY FRUSTRATED	① ② ③ ④ ⑤ ⑥ ⑦ ⑧ ⑨ ⑩
UNABLE TO HOLD BACK EMOTIONS	① ② ③ ④ ⑤ ⑥ ⑦ ⑧ ⑨ ⑩

MEALS

MEDICATIONS

Water Tracker 🍼 🍼 🍼 🍼 🍼 🍼 🍼

NOTES

....
....

DAY GOALS	
1	DATE
2	WEEK
3	LOCATION
	WEIGHT

Mood Tracker 😔 😐 😖 😢 😠 😃

BEHAVIOR

INATTENTION

SHORT ATTENTION	① ② ③ ④ ⑤ ⑥ ⑦ ⑧ ⑨ ⑩
UNMOTIVATED / BORED	① ② ③ ④ ⑤ ⑥ ⑦ ⑧ ⑨ ⑩
SHORT ATTENTION	① ② ③ ④ ⑤ ⑥ ⑦ ⑧ ⑨ ⑩
FORGETFUL / CONFUSIONED	① ② ③ ④ ⑤ ⑥ ⑦ ⑧ ⑨ ⑩

HYPERACTIVITY

CONSTANTLY MOVING / TALKING	① ② ③ ④ ⑤ ⑥ ⑦ ⑧ ⑨ ⑩
STRUGGLING TO SIT STILL	① ② ③ ④ ⑤ ⑥ ⑦ ⑧ ⑨ ⑩
TOUCHING THINGS REPEATEDLY	① ② ③ ④ ⑤ ⑥ ⑦ ⑧ ⑨ ⑩
DIFFICULT SLEEPING	① ② ③ ④ ⑤ ⑥ ⑦ ⑧ ⑨ ⑩

IMPULSIVITY

ACTING WITHOUT THINKING	① ② ③ ④ ⑤ ⑥ ⑦ ⑧ ⑨ ⑩
INTERRUPTING OTHERS	① ② ③ ④ ⑤ ⑥ ⑦ ⑧ ⑨ ⑩
EASILY FRUSTRATED	① ② ③ ④ ⑤ ⑥ ⑦ ⑧ ⑨ ⑩
UNABLE TO HOLD BACK EMOTIONS	① ② ③ ④ ⑤ ⑥ ⑦ ⑧ ⑨ ⑩

MEALS	MEDICATIONS

Water Tracker 🍼 🍼 🍼 🍼 🍼 🍼 🍼 🍼

NOTES

....
....

DAY GOALS

1 ....
2 ....
3 ....

DATE
WEEK
LOCATION
WEIGHT

Mood Tracker 😟 😐 😖 😢 😠 😃

BEHAVIOR

INATTENTION

SHORT ATTENTION	① ② ③ ④ ⑤ ⑥ ⑦ ⑧ ⑨ ⑩
UNMOTIVATED / BORED	① ② ③ ④ ⑤ ⑥ ⑦ ⑧ ⑨ ⑩
SHORT ATTENTION	① ② ③ ④ ⑤ ⑥ ⑦ ⑧ ⑨ ⑩
FORGETFUL / CONFUSIONED	① ② ③ ④ ⑤ ⑥ ⑦ ⑧ ⑨ ⑩

HYPERACTIVITY

CONSTANTLY MOVING / TALKING	① ② ③ ④ ⑤ ⑥ ⑦ ⑧ ⑨ ⑩
STRUGGLING TO SIT STILL	① ② ③ ④ ⑤ ⑥ ⑦ ⑧ ⑨ ⑩
TOUCHING THINGS REPEATEDLY	① ② ③ ④ ⑤ ⑥ ⑦ ⑧ ⑨ ⑩
DIFFICULT SLEEPING	① ② ③ ④ ⑤ ⑥ ⑦ ⑧ ⑨ ⑩

IMPULSIVITY

ACTING WITHOUT THINKING	① ② ③ ④ ⑤ ⑥ ⑦ ⑧ ⑨ ⑩
INTERRUPTING OTHERS	① ② ③ ④ ⑤ ⑥ ⑦ ⑧ ⑨ ⑩
EASILY FRUSTRATED	① ② ③ ④ ⑤ ⑥ ⑦ ⑧ ⑨ ⑩
UNABLE TO HOLD BACK EMOTIONS	① ② ③ ④ ⑤ ⑥ ⑦ ⑧ ⑨ ⑩

MEALS

MEDICATIONS

Water Tracker 🍼 🍼 🍼 🍼 🍼 🍼 🍼

NOTES

....
....

DAY GOALS	
1	
2	
3	

DATE
WEEK
LOCATION
WEIGHT

Mood Tracker 😕 😐 😖 🥲 😠 😃

BEHAVIOR

INATTENTION

SHORT ATTENTION	① ② ③ ④ ⑤ ⑥ ⑦ ⑧ ⑨ ⑩
UNMOTIVATED / BORED	① ② ③ ④ ⑤ ⑥ ⑦ ⑧ ⑨ ⑩
SHORT ATTENTION	① ② ③ ④ ⑤ ⑥ ⑦ ⑧ ⑨ ⑩
FORGETFUL / CONFUSIONED	① ② ③ ④ ⑤ ⑥ ⑦ ⑧ ⑨ ⑩

HYPERACTIVITY

CONSTANTLY MOVING / TALKING	① ② ③ ④ ⑤ ⑥ ⑦ ⑧ ⑨ ⑩
STRUGGLING TO SIT STILL	① ② ③ ④ ⑤ ⑥ ⑦ ⑧ ⑨ ⑩
TOUCHING THINGS REPEATEDLY	① ② ③ ④ ⑤ ⑥ ⑦ ⑧ ⑨ ⑩
DIFFICULT SLEEPING	① ② ③ ④ ⑤ ⑥ ⑦ ⑧ ⑨ ⑩

IMPULSIVITY

ACTING WITHOUT THINKING	① ② ③ ④ ⑤ ⑥ ⑦ ⑧ ⑨ ⑩
INTERRUPTING OTHERS	① ② ③ ④ ⑤ ⑥ ⑦ ⑧ ⑨ ⑩
EASILY FRUSTRATED	① ② ③ ④ ⑤ ⑥ ⑦ ⑧ ⑨ ⑩
UNABLE TO HOLD BACK EMOTIONS	① ② ③ ④ ⑤ ⑥ ⑦ ⑧ ⑨ ⑩

MEALS	MEDICATIONS

Water Tracker 🍼 🍼 🍼 🍼 🍼 🍼 🍼

NOTES

....
....

DAY GOALS		DATE	
1	....	WEEK	
2	....	LOCATION	
3	....	WEIGHT	

Mood Tracker ☹ 😐 😖 😢 😠 😃

BEHAVIOR

INATTENTION

SHORT ATTENTION	① ② ③ ④ ⑤ ⑥ ⑦ ⑧ ⑨ ⑩
UNMOTIVATED / BORED	① ② ③ ④ ⑤ ⑥ ⑦ ⑧ ⑨ ⑩
SHORT ATTENTION	① ② ③ ④ ⑤ ⑥ ⑦ ⑧ ⑨ ⑩
FORGETFUL / CONFUSIONED	① ② ③ ④ ⑤ ⑥ ⑦ ⑧ ⑨ ⑩

HYPERACTIVITY

CONSTANTLY MOVING / TALKING	① ② ③ ④ ⑤ ⑥ ⑦ ⑧ ⑨ ⑩
STRUGGLING TO SIT STILL	① ② ③ ④ ⑤ ⑥ ⑦ ⑧ ⑨ ⑩
TOUCHING THINGS REPEATEDLY	① ② ③ ④ ⑤ ⑥ ⑦ ⑧ ⑨ ⑩
DIFFICULT SLEEPING	① ② ③ ④ ⑤ ⑥ ⑦ ⑧ ⑨ ⑩

IMPULSIVITY

ACTING WITHOUT THINKING	① ② ③ ④ ⑤ ⑥ ⑦ ⑧ ⑨ ⑩
INTERRUPTING OTHERS	① ② ③ ④ ⑤ ⑥ ⑦ ⑧ ⑨ ⑩
EASILY FRUSTRATED	① ② ③ ④ ⑤ ⑥ ⑦ ⑧ ⑨ ⑩
UNABLE TO HOLD BACK EMOTIONS	① ② ③ ④ ⑤ ⑥ ⑦ ⑧ ⑨ ⑩

MEALS	MEDICATIONS

Water Tracker 🍼 🍼 🍼 🍼 🍼 🍼 🍼

NOTES

....
....

DAY GOALS
1 ....
2 ....
3 ....

DATE
WEEK
LOCATION
WEIGHT

Mood Tracker

BEHAVIOR

INATTENTION

SHORT ATTENTION	① ② ③ ④ ⑤ ⑥ ⑦ ⑧ ⑨ ⑩
UNMOTIVATED / BORED	① ② ③ ④ ⑤ ⑥ ⑦ ⑧ ⑨ ⑩
SHORT ATTENTION	① ② ③ ④ ⑤ ⑥ ⑦ ⑧ ⑨ ⑩
FORGETFUL / CONFUSIONED	① ② ③ ④ ⑤ ⑥ ⑦ ⑧ ⑨ ⑩

HYPERACTIVITY

CONSTANTLY MOVING / TALKING	① ② ③ ④ ⑤ ⑥ ⑦ ⑧ ⑨ ⑩
STRUGGLING TO SIT STILL	① ② ③ ④ ⑤ ⑥ ⑦ ⑧ ⑨ ⑩
TOUCHING THINGS REPEATEDLY	① ② ③ ④ ⑤ ⑥ ⑦ ⑧ ⑨ ⑩
DIFFICULT SLEEPING	① ② ③ ④ ⑤ ⑥ ⑦ ⑧ ⑨ ⑩

IMPULSIVITY

ACTING WITHOUT THINKING	① ② ③ ④ ⑤ ⑥ ⑦ ⑧ ⑨ ⑩
INTERRUPTING OTHERS	① ② ③ ④ ⑤ ⑥ ⑦ ⑧ ⑨ ⑩
EASILY FRUSTRATED	① ② ③ ④ ⑤ ⑥ ⑦ ⑧ ⑨ ⑩
UNABLE TO HOLD BACK EMOTIONS	① ② ③ ④ ⑤ ⑥ ⑦ ⑧ ⑨ ⑩

MEALS	MEDICATIONS

Water Tracker

NOTES

....
....

DAY GOALS	DATE
1	WEEK
2	LOCATION
3	WEIGHT

Mood Tracker ☹ 😐 😖 😢 😠 😃

BEHAVIOR

INATTENTION

SHORT ATTENTION	① ② ③ ④ ⑤ ⑥ ⑦ ⑧ ⑨ ⑩
UNMOTIVATED / BORED	① ② ③ ④ ⑤ ⑥ ⑦ ⑧ ⑨ ⑩
SHORT ATTENTION	① ② ③ ④ ⑤ ⑥ ⑦ ⑧ ⑨ ⑩
FORGETFUL / CONFUSIONED	① ② ③ ④ ⑤ ⑥ ⑦ ⑧ ⑨ ⑩

HYPERACTIVITY

CONSTANTLY MOVING / TALKING	① ② ③ ④ ⑤ ⑥ ⑦ ⑧ ⑨ ⑩
STRUGGLING TO SIT STILL	① ② ③ ④ ⑤ ⑥ ⑦ ⑧ ⑨ ⑩
TOUCHING THINGS REPEATEDLY	① ② ③ ④ ⑤ ⑥ ⑦ ⑧ ⑨ ⑩
DIFFICULT SLEEPING	① ② ③ ④ ⑤ ⑥ ⑦ ⑧ ⑨ ⑩

IMPULSIVITY

ACTING WITHOUT THINKING	① ② ③ ④ ⑤ ⑥ ⑦ ⑧ ⑨ ⑩
INTERRUPTING OTHERS	① ② ③ ④ ⑤ ⑥ ⑦ ⑧ ⑨ ⑩
EASILY FRUSTRATED	① ② ③ ④ ⑤ ⑥ ⑦ ⑧ ⑨ ⑩
UNABLE TO HOLD BACK EMOTIONS	① ② ③ ④ ⑤ ⑥ ⑦ ⑧ ⑨ ⑩

MEALS	MEDICATIONS

Water Tracker 🍼 🍼 🍼 🍼 🍼 🍼 🍼

NOTES

....
....

DAY GOALS

1 ....
2 ....
3 ....

DATE
WEEK
LOCATION
WEIGHT

Mood Tracker ☹ 😐 😖 😢 😠 😃

BEHAVIOR

INATTENTION

SHORT ATTENTION	① ② ③ ④ ⑤ ⑥ ⑦ ⑧ ⑨ ⑩
UNMOTIVATED / BORED	① ② ③ ④ ⑤ ⑥ ⑦ ⑧ ⑨ ⑩
SHORT ATTENTION	① ② ③ ④ ⑤ ⑥ ⑦ ⑧ ⑨ ⑩
FORGETFUL / CONFUSIONED	① ② ③ ④ ⑤ ⑥ ⑦ ⑧ ⑨ ⑩

HYPERACTIVITY

CONSTANTLY MOVING / TALKING	① ② ③ ④ ⑤ ⑥ ⑦ ⑧ ⑨ ⑩
STRUGGLING TO SIT STILL	① ② ③ ④ ⑤ ⑥ ⑦ ⑧ ⑨ ⑩
TOUCHING THINGS REPEATEDLY	① ② ③ ④ ⑤ ⑥ ⑦ ⑧ ⑨ ⑩
DIFFICULT SLEEPING	① ② ③ ④ ⑤ ⑥ ⑦ ⑧ ⑨ ⑩

IMPULSIVITY

ACTING WITHOUT THINKING	① ② ③ ④ ⑤ ⑥ ⑦ ⑧ ⑨ ⑩
INTERRUPTING OTHERS	① ② ③ ④ ⑤ ⑥ ⑦ ⑧ ⑨ ⑩
EASILY FRUSTRATED	① ② ③ ④ ⑤ ⑥ ⑦ ⑧ ⑨ ⑩
UNABLE TO HOLD BACK EMOTIONS	① ② ③ ④ ⑤ ⑥ ⑦ ⑧ ⑨ ⑩

MEALS

MEDICATIONS

Water Tracker 🍼 🍼 🍼 🍼 🍼 🍼 🍼

NOTES

....
....

DAY GOALS

1 ....
2 ....
3 ....

DATE
WEEK
LOCATION
WEIGHT

Mood Tracker

BEHAVIOR

INATTENTION

SHORT ATTENTION	① ② ③ ④ ⑤ ⑥ ⑦ ⑧ ⑨ ⑩
UNMOTIVATED / BORED	① ② ③ ④ ⑤ ⑥ ⑦ ⑧ ⑨ ⑩
SHORT ATTENTION	① ② ③ ④ ⑤ ⑥ ⑦ ⑧ ⑨ ⑩
FORGETFUL / CONFUSIONED	① ② ③ ④ ⑤ ⑥ ⑦ ⑧ ⑨ ⑩

HYPERACTIVITY

CONSTANTLY MOVING / TALKING	① ② ③ ④ ⑤ ⑥ ⑦ ⑧ ⑨ ⑩
STRUGGLING TO SIT STILL	① ② ③ ④ ⑤ ⑥ ⑦ ⑧ ⑨ ⑩
TOUCHING THINGS REPEATEDLY	① ② ③ ④ ⑤ ⑥ ⑦ ⑧ ⑨ ⑩
DIFFICULT SLEEPING	① ② ③ ④ ⑤ ⑥ ⑦ ⑧ ⑨ ⑩

IMPULSIVITY

ACTING WITHOUT THINKING	① ② ③ ④ ⑤ ⑥ ⑦ ⑧ ⑨ ⑩
INTERRUPTING OTHERS	① ② ③ ④ ⑤ ⑥ ⑦ ⑧ ⑨ ⑩
EASILY FRUSTRATED	① ② ③ ④ ⑤ ⑥ ⑦ ⑧ ⑨ ⑩
UNABLE TO HOLD BACK EMOTIONS	① ② ③ ④ ⑤ ⑥ ⑦ ⑧ ⑨ ⑩

MEALS

MEDICATIONS

Water Tracker

NOTES

....
....

DAY GOALS

1 ....
2 ....
3 ....

DATE
WEEK
LOCATION
WEIGHT

Mood Tracker 😕 😐 😖 😢 😠 😃

BEHAVIOR

INATTENTION

SHORT ATTENTION	① ② ③ ④ ⑤ ⑥ ⑦ ⑧ ⑨ ⑩
UNMOTIVATED / BORED	① ② ③ ④ ⑤ ⑥ ⑦ ⑧ ⑨ ⑩
SHORT ATTENTION	① ② ③ ④ ⑤ ⑥ ⑦ ⑧ ⑨ ⑩
FORGETFUL / CONFUSIONED	① ② ③ ④ ⑤ ⑥ ⑦ ⑧ ⑨ ⑩

HYPERACTIVITY

CONSTANTLY MOVING / TALKING	① ② ③ ④ ⑤ ⑥ ⑦ ⑧ ⑨ ⑩
STRUGGLING TO SIT STILL	① ② ③ ④ ⑤ ⑥ ⑦ ⑧ ⑨ ⑩
TOUCHING THINGS REPEATEDLY	① ② ③ ④ ⑤ ⑥ ⑦ ⑧ ⑨ ⑩
DIFFICULT SLEEPING	① ② ③ ④ ⑤ ⑥ ⑦ ⑧ ⑨ ⑩

IMPULSIVITY

ACTING WITHOUT THINKING	① ② ③ ④ ⑤ ⑥ ⑦ ⑧ ⑨ ⑩
INTERRUPTING OTHERS	① ② ③ ④ ⑤ ⑥ ⑦ ⑧ ⑨ ⑩
EASILY FRUSTRATED	① ② ③ ④ ⑤ ⑥ ⑦ ⑧ ⑨ ⑩
UNABLE TO HOLD BACK EMOTIONS	① ② ③ ④ ⑤ ⑥ ⑦ ⑧ ⑨ ⑩

MEALS

MEDICATIONS

Water Tracker 🍼 🍼 🍼 🍼 🍼 🍼 🍼

NOTES

....
....

DAY GOALS

1 ....
2 ....
3 ....

DATE
WEEK
LOCATION
WEIGHT

Mood Tracker ☹ 😐 😖 😢 😠 😃

BEHAVIOR

INATTENTION

SHORT ATTENTION	① ② ③ ④ ⑤ ⑥ ⑦ ⑧ ⑨ ⑩
UNMOTIVATED / BORED	① ② ③ ④ ⑤ ⑥ ⑦ ⑧ ⑨ ⑩
SHORT ATTENTION	① ② ③ ④ ⑤ ⑥ ⑦ ⑧ ⑨ ⑩
FORGETFUL / CONFUSIONED	① ② ③ ④ ⑤ ⑥ ⑦ ⑧ ⑨ ⑩

HYPERACTIVITY

CONSTANTLY MOVING / TALKING	① ② ③ ④ ⑤ ⑥ ⑦ ⑧ ⑨ ⑩
STRUGGLING TO SIT STILL	① ② ③ ④ ⑤ ⑥ ⑦ ⑧ ⑨ ⑩
TOUCHING THINGS REPEATEDLY	① ② ③ ④ ⑤ ⑥ ⑦ ⑧ ⑨ ⑩
DIFFICULT SLEEPING	① ② ③ ④ ⑤ ⑥ ⑦ ⑧ ⑨ ⑩

IMPULSIVITY

ACTING WITHOUT THINKING	① ② ③ ④ ⑤ ⑥ ⑦ ⑧ ⑨ ⑩
INTERRUPTING OTHERS	① ② ③ ④ ⑤ ⑥ ⑦ ⑧ ⑨ ⑩
EASILY FRUSTRATED	① ② ③ ④ ⑤ ⑥ ⑦ ⑧ ⑨ ⑩
UNABLE TO HOLD BACK EMOTIONS	① ② ③ ④ ⑤ ⑥ ⑦ ⑧ ⑨ ⑩

MEALS

MEDICATIONS

Water Tracker 🍶 🍶 🍶 🍶 🍶 🍶 🍶 🍶

NOTES

....
....

DAY GOALS	
1	DATE
2	WEEK
3	LOCATION
	WEIGHT

Mood Tracker

BEHAVIOR

INATTENTION

SHORT ATTENTION	① ② ③ ④ ⑤ ⑥ ⑦ ⑧ ⑨ ⑩
UNMOTIVATED / BORED	① ② ③ ④ ⑤ ⑥ ⑦ ⑧ ⑨ ⑩
SHORT ATTENTION	① ② ③ ④ ⑤ ⑥ ⑦ ⑧ ⑨ ⑩
FORGETFUL / CONFUSIONED	① ② ③ ④ ⑤ ⑥ ⑦ ⑧ ⑨ ⑩

HYPERACTIVITY

CONSTANTLY MOVING / TALKING	① ② ③ ④ ⑤ ⑥ ⑦ ⑧ ⑨ ⑩
STRUGGLING TO SIT STILL	① ② ③ ④ ⑤ ⑥ ⑦ ⑧ ⑨ ⑩
TOUCHING THINGS REPEATEDLY	① ② ③ ④ ⑤ ⑥ ⑦ ⑧ ⑨ ⑩
DIFFICULT SLEEPING	① ② ③ ④ ⑤ ⑥ ⑦ ⑧ ⑨ ⑩

IMPULSIVITY

ACTING WITHOUT THINKING	① ② ③ ④ ⑤ ⑥ ⑦ ⑧ ⑨ ⑩
INTERRUPTING OTHERS	① ② ③ ④ ⑤ ⑥ ⑦ ⑧ ⑨ ⑩
EASILY FRUSTRATED	① ② ③ ④ ⑤ ⑥ ⑦ ⑧ ⑨ ⑩
UNABLE TO HOLD BACK EMOTIONS	① ② ③ ④ ⑤ ⑥ ⑦ ⑧ ⑨ ⑩

MEALS	MEDICATIONS

Water Tracker

NOTES

....
....

DAY GOALS

1 ....
2 ....
3 ....

DATE
WEEK
LOCATION
WEIGHT

Mood Tracker

BEHAVIOR

INATTENTION

Behavior	Rating
SHORT ATTENTION	① ② ③ ④ ⑤ ⑥ ⑦ ⑧ ⑨ ⑩
UNMOTIVATED / BORED	① ② ③ ④ ⑤ ⑥ ⑦ ⑧ ⑨ ⑩
SHORT ATTENTION	① ② ③ ④ ⑤ ⑥ ⑦ ⑧ ⑨ ⑩
FORGETFUL / CONFUSIONED	① ② ③ ④ ⑤ ⑥ ⑦ ⑧ ⑨ ⑩

HYPERACTIVITY

Behavior	Rating
CONSTANTLY MOVING / TALKING	① ② ③ ④ ⑤ ⑥ ⑦ ⑧ ⑨ ⑩
STRUGGLING TO SIT STILL	① ② ③ ④ ⑤ ⑥ ⑦ ⑧ ⑨ ⑩
TOUCHING THINGS REPEATEDLY	① ② ③ ④ ⑤ ⑥ ⑦ ⑧ ⑨ ⑩
DIFFICULT SLEEPING	① ② ③ ④ ⑤ ⑥ ⑦ ⑧ ⑨ ⑩

IMPULSIVITY

Behavior	Rating
ACTING WITHOUT THINKING	① ② ③ ④ ⑤ ⑥ ⑦ ⑧ ⑨ ⑩
INTERRUPTING OTHERS	① ② ③ ④ ⑤ ⑥ ⑦ ⑧ ⑨ ⑩
EASILY FRUSTRATED	① ② ③ ④ ⑤ ⑥ ⑦ ⑧ ⑨ ⑩
UNABLE TO HOLD BACK EMOTIONS	① ② ③ ④ ⑤ ⑥ ⑦ ⑧ ⑨ ⑩

MEALS

MEDICATIONS

Water Tracker

NOTES

....
....

DAY GOALS

1 ....
2 ....
3 ....

DATE
WEEK
LOCATION
WEIGHT

Mood Tracker ☹ 😐 😖 😢 😠 😃

BEHAVIOR

INATTENTION

SHORT ATTENTION	① ② ③ ④ ⑤ ⑥ ⑦ ⑧ ⑨ ⑩
UNMOTIVATED / BORED	① ② ③ ④ ⑤ ⑥ ⑦ ⑧ ⑨ ⑩
SHORT ATTENTION	① ② ③ ④ ⑤ ⑥ ⑦ ⑧ ⑨ ⑩
FORGETFUL / CONFUSIONED	① ② ③ ④ ⑤ ⑥ ⑦ ⑧ ⑨ ⑩

HYPERACTIVITY

CONSTANTLY MOVING / TALKING	① ② ③ ④ ⑤ ⑥ ⑦ ⑧ ⑨ ⑩
STRUGGLING TO SIT STILL	① ② ③ ④ ⑤ ⑥ ⑦ ⑧ ⑨ ⑩
TOUCHING THINGS REPEATEDLY	① ② ③ ④ ⑤ ⑥ ⑦ ⑧ ⑨ ⑩
DIFFICULT SLEEPING	① ② ③ ④ ⑤ ⑥ ⑦ ⑧ ⑨ ⑩

IMPULSIVITY

ACTING WITHOUT THINKING	① ② ③ ④ ⑤ ⑥ ⑦ ⑧ ⑨ ⑩
INTERRUPTING OTHERS	① ② ③ ④ ⑤ ⑥ ⑦ ⑧ ⑨ ⑩
EASILY FRUSTRATED	① ② ③ ④ ⑤ ⑥ ⑦ ⑧ ⑨ ⑩
UNABLE TO HOLD BACK EMOTIONS	① ② ③ ④ ⑤ ⑥ ⑦ ⑧ ⑨ ⑩

MEALS

MEDICATIONS

Water Tracker 🍼 🍼 🍼 🍼 🍼 🍼 🍼

NOTES

....
....

DAY GOALS

1 ....
2 ....
3 ....

DATE
WEEK
LOCATION
WEIGHT

Mood Tracker

BEHAVIOR

INATTENTION

SHORT ATTENTION	① ② ③ ④ ⑤ ⑥ ⑦ ⑧ ⑨ ⑩
UNMOTIVATED / BORED	① ② ③ ④ ⑤ ⑥ ⑦ ⑧ ⑨ ⑩
SHORT ATTENTION	① ② ③ ④ ⑤ ⑥ ⑦ ⑧ ⑨ ⑩
FORGETFUL / CONFUSIONED	① ② ③ ④ ⑤ ⑥ ⑦ ⑧ ⑨ ⑩

HYPERACTIVITY

CONSTANTLY MOVING / TALKING	① ② ③ ④ ⑤ ⑥ ⑦ ⑧ ⑨ ⑩
STRUGGLING TO SIT STILL	① ② ③ ④ ⑤ ⑥ ⑦ ⑧ ⑨ ⑩
TOUCHING THINGS REPEATEDLY	① ② ③ ④ ⑤ ⑥ ⑦ ⑧ ⑨ ⑩
DIFFICULT SLEEPING	① ② ③ ④ ⑤ ⑥ ⑦ ⑧ ⑨ ⑩

IMPULSIVITY

ACTING WITHOUT THINKING	① ② ③ ④ ⑤ ⑥ ⑦ ⑧ ⑨ ⑩
INTERRUPTING OTHERS	① ② ③ ④ ⑤ ⑥ ⑦ ⑧ ⑨ ⑩
EASILY FRUSTRATED	① ② ③ ④ ⑤ ⑥ ⑦ ⑧ ⑨ ⑩
UNABLE TO HOLD BACK EMOTIONS	① ② ③ ④ ⑤ ⑥ ⑦ ⑧ ⑨ ⑩

MEALS

MEDICATIONS

Water Tracker

NOTES

....
....

DAY GOALS	
1	
2	
3	

DATE
WEEK
LOCATION
WEIGHT

Mood Tracker 😟 😐 😖 😢 😠 😃

BEHAVIOR

INATTENTION

SHORT ATTENTION	① ② ③ ④ ⑤ ⑥ ⑦ ⑧ ⑨ ⑩
UNMOTIVATED / BORED	① ② ③ ④ ⑤ ⑥ ⑦ ⑧ ⑨ ⑩
SHORT ATTENTION	① ② ③ ④ ⑤ ⑥ ⑦ ⑧ ⑨ ⑩
FORGETFUL / CONFUSIONED	① ② ③ ④ ⑤ ⑥ ⑦ ⑧ ⑨ ⑩

HYPERACTIVITY

CONSTANTLY MOVING / TALKING	① ② ③ ④ ⑤ ⑥ ⑦ ⑧ ⑨ ⑩
STRUGGLING TO SIT STILL	① ② ③ ④ ⑤ ⑥ ⑦ ⑧ ⑨ ⑩
TOUCHING THINGS REPEATEDLY	① ② ③ ④ ⑤ ⑥ ⑦ ⑧ ⑨ ⑩
DIFFICULT SLEEPING	① ② ③ ④ ⑤ ⑥ ⑦ ⑧ ⑨ ⑩

IMPULSIVITY

ACTING WITHOUT THINKING	① ② ③ ④ ⑤ ⑥ ⑦ ⑧ ⑨ ⑩
INTERRUPTING OTHERS	① ② ③ ④ ⑤ ⑥ ⑦ ⑧ ⑨ ⑩
EASILY FRUSTRATED	① ② ③ ④ ⑤ ⑥ ⑦ ⑧ ⑨ ⑩
UNABLE TO HOLD BACK EMOTIONS	① ② ③ ④ ⑤ ⑥ ⑦ ⑧ ⑨ ⑩

MEALS	MEDICATIONS

Water Tracker 🍼 🍼 🍼 🍼 🍼 🍼 🍼

NOTES

....
....

DAY GOALS	
1	
2	
3	

DATE
WEEK
LOCATION
WEIGHT

Mood Tracker 😕 😐 🤢 😢 😠 😃

BEHAVIOR

INATTENTION

SHORT ATTENTION	① ② ③ ④ ⑤ ⑥ ⑦ ⑧ ⑨ ⑩
UNMOTIVATED / BORED	① ② ③ ④ ⑤ ⑥ ⑦ ⑧ ⑨ ⑩
SHORT ATTENTION	① ② ③ ④ ⑤ ⑥ ⑦ ⑧ ⑨ ⑩
FORGETFUL / CONFUSIONED	① ② ③ ④ ⑤ ⑥ ⑦ ⑧ ⑨ ⑩

HYPERACTIVITY

CONSTANTLY MOVING / TALKING	① ② ③ ④ ⑤ ⑥ ⑦ ⑧ ⑨ ⑩
STRUGGLING TO SIT STILL	① ② ③ ④ ⑤ ⑥ ⑦ ⑧ ⑨ ⑩
TOUCHING THINGS REPEATEDLY	① ② ③ ④ ⑤ ⑥ ⑦ ⑧ ⑨ ⑩
DIFFICULT SLEEPING	① ② ③ ④ ⑤ ⑥ ⑦ ⑧ ⑨ ⑩

IMPULSIVITY

ACTING WITHOUT THINKING	① ② ③ ④ ⑤ ⑥ ⑦ ⑧ ⑨ ⑩
INTERRUPTING OTHERS	① ② ③ ④ ⑤ ⑥ ⑦ ⑧ ⑨ ⑩
EASILY FRUSTRATED	① ② ③ ④ ⑤ ⑥ ⑦ ⑧ ⑨ ⑩
UNABLE TO HOLD BACK EMOTIONS	① ② ③ ④ ⑤ ⑥ ⑦ ⑧ ⑨ ⑩

MEALS	MEDICATIONS

Water Tracker 🍼 🍼 🍼 🍼 🍼 🍼 🍼

NOTES

....
....

DAY GOALS	
1	DATE
2	WEEK
3	LOCATION
	WEIGHT

Mood Tracker ☹️ 😐 😖 😢 😠 😃

BEHAVIOR

INATTENTION

SHORT ATTENTION	① ② ③ ④ ⑤ ⑥ ⑦ ⑧ ⑨ ⑩
UNMOTIVATED / BORED	① ② ③ ④ ⑤ ⑥ ⑦ ⑧ ⑨ ⑩
SHORT ATTENTION	① ② ③ ④ ⑤ ⑥ ⑦ ⑧ ⑨ ⑩
FORGETFUL / CONFUSIONED	① ② ③ ④ ⑤ ⑥ ⑦ ⑧ ⑨ ⑩

HYPERACTIVITY

CONSTANTLY MOVING / TALKING	① ② ③ ④ ⑤ ⑥ ⑦ ⑧ ⑨ ⑩
STRUGGLING TO SIT STILL	① ② ③ ④ ⑤ ⑥ ⑦ ⑧ ⑨ ⑩
TOUCHING THINGS REPEATEDLY	① ② ③ ④ ⑤ ⑥ ⑦ ⑧ ⑨ ⑩
DIFFICULT SLEEPING	① ② ③ ④ ⑤ ⑥ ⑦ ⑧ ⑨ ⑩

IMPULSIVITY

ACTING WITHOUT THINKING	① ② ③ ④ ⑤ ⑥ ⑦ ⑧ ⑨ ⑩
INTERRUPTING OTHERS	① ② ③ ④ ⑤ ⑥ ⑦ ⑧ ⑨ ⑩
EASILY FRUSTRATED	① ② ③ ④ ⑤ ⑥ ⑦ ⑧ ⑨ ⑩
UNABLE TO HOLD BACK EMOTIONS	① ② ③ ④ ⑤ ⑥ ⑦ ⑧ ⑨ ⑩

MEALS	MEDICATIONS

Water Tracker 🍼 🍼 🍼 🍼 🍼 🍼 🍼

NOTES

....
....

DAY GOALS	
1	
2	
3	

DATE
WEEK
LOCATION
WEIGHT

Mood Tracker 😕 😐 😖 😢 😠 😃

BEHAVIOR

INATTENTION

SHORT ATTENTION	① ② ③ ④ ⑤ ⑥ ⑦ ⑧ ⑨ ⑩
UNMOTIVATED / BORED	① ② ③ ④ ⑤ ⑥ ⑦ ⑧ ⑨ ⑩
SHORT ATTENTION	① ② ③ ④ ⑤ ⑥ ⑦ ⑧ ⑨ ⑩
FORGETFUL / CONFUSIONED	① ② ③ ④ ⑤ ⑥ ⑦ ⑧ ⑨ ⑩

HYPERACTIVITY

CONSTANTLY MOVING / TALKING	① ② ③ ④ ⑤ ⑥ ⑦ ⑧ ⑨ ⑩
STRUGGLING TO SIT STILL	① ② ③ ④ ⑤ ⑥ ⑦ ⑧ ⑨ ⑩
TOUCHING THINGS REPEATEDLY	① ② ③ ④ ⑤ ⑥ ⑦ ⑧ ⑨ ⑩
DIFFICULT SLEEPING	① ② ③ ④ ⑤ ⑥ ⑦ ⑧ ⑨ ⑩

IMPULSIVITY

ACTING WITHOUT THINKING	① ② ③ ④ ⑤ ⑥ ⑦ ⑧ ⑨ ⑩
INTERRUPTING OTHERS	① ② ③ ④ ⑤ ⑥ ⑦ ⑧ ⑨ ⑩
EASILY FRUSTRATED	① ② ③ ④ ⑤ ⑥ ⑦ ⑧ ⑨ ⑩
UNABLE TO HOLD BACK EMOTIONS	① ② ③ ④ ⑤ ⑥ ⑦ ⑧ ⑨ ⑩

MEALS	MEDICATIONS

Water Tracker 🍼 🍼 🍼 🍼 🍼 🍼 🍼

NOTES

....
....

DAY GOALS

1 ....
2 ....
3 ....

DATE
WEEK
LOCATION
WEIGHT

Mood Tracker 😕 😐 😖 😢 😠 😃

BEHAVIOR

INATTENTION

Behavior	Rating
SHORT ATTENTION	① ② ③ ④ ⑤ ⑥ ⑦ ⑧ ⑨ ⑩
UNMOTIVATED / BORED	① ② ③ ④ ⑤ ⑥ ⑦ ⑧ ⑨ ⑩
SHORT ATTENTION	① ② ③ ④ ⑤ ⑥ ⑦ ⑧ ⑨ ⑩
FORGETFUL / CONFUSIONED	① ② ③ ④ ⑤ ⑥ ⑦ ⑧ ⑨ ⑩

HYPERACTIVITY

Behavior	Rating
CONSTANTLY MOVING / TALKING	① ② ③ ④ ⑤ ⑥ ⑦ ⑧ ⑨ ⑩
STRUGGLING TO SIT STILL	① ② ③ ④ ⑤ ⑥ ⑦ ⑧ ⑨ ⑩
TOUCHING THINGS REPEATEDLY	① ② ③ ④ ⑤ ⑥ ⑦ ⑧ ⑨ ⑩
DIFFICULT SLEEPING	① ② ③ ④ ⑤ ⑥ ⑦ ⑧ ⑨ ⑩

IMPULSIVITY

Behavior	Rating
ACTING WITHOUT THINKING	① ② ③ ④ ⑤ ⑥ ⑦ ⑧ ⑨ ⑩
INTERRUPTING OTHERS	① ② ③ ④ ⑤ ⑥ ⑦ ⑧ ⑨ ⑩
EASILY FRUSTRATED	① ② ③ ④ ⑤ ⑥ ⑦ ⑧ ⑨ ⑩
UNABLE TO HOLD BACK EMOTIONS	① ② ③ ④ ⑤ ⑥ ⑦ ⑧ ⑨ ⑩

MEALS

MEDICATIONS

Water Tracker 🍶 🍶 🍶 🍶 🍶 🍶 🍶

NOTES

....
....

DAY GOALS
1 ....
2 ....
3 ....

DATE
WEEK
LOCATION
WEIGHT

Mood Tracker 🙁 😐 😖 😢 😠 😃

BEHAVIOR

INATTENTION

SHORT ATTENTION	① ② ③ ④ ⑤ ⑥ ⑦ ⑧ ⑨ ⑩
UNMOTIVATED / BORED	① ② ③ ④ ⑤ ⑥ ⑦ ⑧ ⑨ ⑩
SHORT ATTENTION	① ② ③ ④ ⑤ ⑥ ⑦ ⑧ ⑨ ⑩
FORGETFUL / CONFUSIONED	① ② ③ ④ ⑤ ⑥ ⑦ ⑧ ⑨ ⑩

HYPERACTIVITY

CONSTANTLY MOVING / TALKING	① ② ③ ④ ⑤ ⑥ ⑦ ⑧ ⑨ ⑩
STRUGGLING TO SIT STILL	① ② ③ ④ ⑤ ⑥ ⑦ ⑧ ⑨ ⑩
TOUCHING THINGS REPEATEDLY	① ② ③ ④ ⑤ ⑥ ⑦ ⑧ ⑨ ⑩
DIFFICULT SLEEPING	① ② ③ ④ ⑤ ⑥ ⑦ ⑧ ⑨ ⑩

IMPULSIVITY

ACTING WITHOUT THINKING	① ② ③ ④ ⑤ ⑥ ⑦ ⑧ ⑨ ⑩
INTERRUPTING OTHERS	① ② ③ ④ ⑤ ⑥ ⑦ ⑧ ⑨ ⑩
EASILY FRUSTRATED	① ② ③ ④ ⑤ ⑥ ⑦ ⑧ ⑨ ⑩
UNABLE TO HOLD BACK EMOTIONS	① ② ③ ④ ⑤ ⑥ ⑦ ⑧ ⑨ ⑩

MEALS	MEDICATIONS

Water Tracker 🍼 🍼 🍼 🍼 🍼 🍼 🍼

NOTES
....
....

DAY GOALS

1 ....
2 ....
3 ....

DATE
WEEK
LOCATION
WEIGHT

Mood Tracker ☹ 😐 😖 😢 😠 😃

BEHAVIOR

INATTENTION

Behavior	Rating
SHORT ATTENTION	① ② ③ ④ ⑤ ⑥ ⑦ ⑧ ⑨ ⑩
UNMOTIVATED / BORED	① ② ③ ④ ⑤ ⑥ ⑦ ⑧ ⑨ ⑩
SHORT ATTENTION	① ② ③ ④ ⑤ ⑥ ⑦ ⑧ ⑨ ⑩
FORGETFUL / CONFUSIONED	① ② ③ ④ ⑤ ⑥ ⑦ ⑧ ⑨ ⑩

HYPERACTIVITY

Behavior	Rating
CONSTANTLY MOVING / TALKING	① ② ③ ④ ⑤ ⑥ ⑦ ⑧ ⑨ ⑩
STRUGGLING TO SIT STILL	① ② ③ ④ ⑤ ⑥ ⑦ ⑧ ⑨ ⑩
TOUCHING THINGS REPEATEDLY	① ② ③ ④ ⑤ ⑥ ⑦ ⑧ ⑨ ⑩
DIFFICULT SLEEPING	① ② ③ ④ ⑤ ⑥ ⑦ ⑧ ⑨ ⑩

IMPULSIVITY

Behavior	Rating
ACTING WITHOUT THINKING	① ② ③ ④ ⑤ ⑥ ⑦ ⑧ ⑨ ⑩
INTERRUPTING OTHERS	① ② ③ ④ ⑤ ⑥ ⑦ ⑧ ⑨ ⑩
EASILY FRUSTRATED	① ② ③ ④ ⑤ ⑥ ⑦ ⑧ ⑨ ⑩
UNABLE TO HOLD BACK EMOTIONS	① ② ③ ④ ⑤ ⑥ ⑦ ⑧ ⑨ ⑩

MEALS

MEDICATIONS

Water Tracker 🥤 🥤 🥤 🥤 🥤 🥤 🥤

NOTES

....
....

DAY GOALS	
1	
2	
3	

DATE
WEEK
LOCATION
WEIGHT

Mood Tracker ☹ 😐 >_< 😢 😠 😃

BEHAVIOR

INATTENTION

SHORT ATTENTION	① ② ③ ④ ⑤ ⑥ ⑦ ⑧ ⑨ ⑩
UNMOTIVATED / BORED	① ② ③ ④ ⑤ ⑥ ⑦ ⑧ ⑨ ⑩
SHORT ATTENTION	① ② ③ ④ ⑤ ⑥ ⑦ ⑧ ⑨ ⑩
FORGETFUL / CONFUSIONED	① ② ③ ④ ⑤ ⑥ ⑦ ⑧ ⑨ ⑩

HYPERACTIVITY

CONSTANTLY MOVING / TALKING	① ② ③ ④ ⑤ ⑥ ⑦ ⑧ ⑨ ⑩
STRUGGLING TO SIT STILL	① ② ③ ④ ⑤ ⑥ ⑦ ⑧ ⑨ ⑩
TOUCHING THINGS REPEATEDLY	① ② ③ ④ ⑤ ⑥ ⑦ ⑧ ⑨ ⑩
DIFFICULT SLEEPING	① ② ③ ④ ⑤ ⑥ ⑦ ⑧ ⑨ ⑩

IMPULSIVITY

ACTING WITHOUT THINKING	① ② ③ ④ ⑤ ⑥ ⑦ ⑧ ⑨ ⑩
INTERRUPTING OTHERS	① ② ③ ④ ⑤ ⑥ ⑦ ⑧ ⑨ ⑩
EASILY FRUSTRATED	① ② ③ ④ ⑤ ⑥ ⑦ ⑧ ⑨ ⑩
UNABLE TO HOLD BACK EMOTIONS	① ② ③ ④ ⑤ ⑥ ⑦ ⑧ ⑨ ⑩

MEALS	MEDICATIONS

Water Tracker 🍶 🍶 🍶 🍶 🍶 🍶 🍶

NOTES

....
....

DAY GOALS		
1	DATE	
2	WEEK	
3	LOCATION	
	WEIGHT	

Mood Tracker 😕 😐 😖 😢 😠 😃

BEHAVIOR

INATTENTION

SHORT ATTENTION	1 2 3 4 5 6 7 8 9 10
UNMOTIVATED / BORED	1 2 3 4 5 6 7 8 9 10
SHORT ATTENTION	1 2 3 4 5 6 7 8 9 10
FORGETFUL / CONFUSIONED	1 2 3 4 5 6 7 8 9 10

HYPERACTIVITY

CONSTANTLY MOVING / TALKING	1 2 3 4 5 6 7 8 9 10
STRUGGLING TO SIT STILL	1 2 3 4 5 6 7 8 9 10
TOUCHING THINGS REPEATEDLY	1 2 3 4 5 6 7 8 9 10
DIFFICULT SLEEPING	1 2 3 4 5 6 7 8 9 10

IMPULSIVITY

ACTING WITHOUT THINKING	1 2 3 4 5 6 7 8 9 10
INTERRUPTING OTHERS	1 2 3 4 5 6 7 8 9 10
EASILY FRUSTRATED	1 2 3 4 5 6 7 8 9 10
UNABLE TO HOLD BACK EMOTIONS	1 2 3 4 5 6 7 8 9 10

MEALS	MEDICATIONS

Water Tracker 🍼 🍼 🍼 🍼 🍼 🍼 🍼

NOTES
....
....

DAY GOALS	
1	
2	
3	

DATE
WEEK
LOCATION
WEIGHT

Mood Tracker   😕 😐 😖 😢 😠 😃

BEHAVIOR

INATTENTION

SHORT ATTENTION	① ② ③ ④ ⑤ ⑥ ⑦ ⑧ ⑨ ⑩
UNMOTIVATED / BORED	① ② ③ ④ ⑤ ⑥ ⑦ ⑧ ⑨ ⑩
SHORT ATTENTION	① ② ③ ④ ⑤ ⑥ ⑦ ⑧ ⑨ ⑩
FORGETFUL / CONFUSIONED	① ② ③ ④ ⑤ ⑥ ⑦ ⑧ ⑨ ⑩

HYPERACTIVITY

CONSTANTLY MOVING / TALKING	① ② ③ ④ ⑤ ⑥ ⑦ ⑧ ⑨ ⑩
STRUGGLING TO SIT STILL	① ② ③ ④ ⑤ ⑥ ⑦ ⑧ ⑨ ⑩
TOUCHING THINGS REPEATEDLY	① ② ③ ④ ⑤ ⑥ ⑦ ⑧ ⑨ ⑩
DIFFICULT SLEEPING	① ② ③ ④ ⑤ ⑥ ⑦ ⑧ ⑨ ⑩

IMPULSIVITY

ACTING WITHOUT THINKING	① ② ③ ④ ⑤ ⑥ ⑦ ⑧ ⑨ ⑩
INTERRUPTING OTHERS	① ② ③ ④ ⑤ ⑥ ⑦ ⑧ ⑨ ⑩
EASILY FRUSTRATED	① ② ③ ④ ⑤ ⑥ ⑦ ⑧ ⑨ ⑩
UNABLE TO HOLD BACK EMOTIONS	① ② ③ ④ ⑤ ⑥ ⑦ ⑧ ⑨ ⑩

MEALS	MEDICATIONS

Water Tracker 🍼 🍼 🍼 🍼 🍼 🍼 🍼

NOTES

....
....

DAY GOALS

1 ....
2 ....
3 ....

DATE
WEEK
LOCATION
WEIGHT

Mood Tracker

BEHAVIOR

INATTENTION

Behavior	Rating
SHORT ATTENTION	1 2 3 4 5 6 7 8 9 10
UNMOTIVATED / BORED	1 2 3 4 5 6 7 8 9 10
SHORT ATTENTION	1 2 3 4 5 6 7 8 9 10
FORGETFUL / CONFUSIONED	1 2 3 4 5 6 7 8 9 10

HYPERACTIVITY

Behavior	Rating
CONSTANTLY MOVING / TALKING	1 2 3 4 5 6 7 8 9 10
STRUGGLING TO SIT STILL	1 2 3 4 5 6 7 8 9 10
TOUCHING THINGS REPEATEDLY	1 2 3 4 5 6 7 8 9 10
DIFFICULT SLEEPING	1 2 3 4 5 6 7 8 9 10

IMPULSIVITY

Behavior	Rating
ACTING WITHOUT THINKING	1 2 3 4 5 6 7 8 9 10
INTERRUPTING OTHERS	1 2 3 4 5 6 7 8 9 10
EASILY FRUSTRATED	1 2 3 4 5 6 7 8 9 10
UNABLE TO HOLD BACK EMOTIONS	1 2 3 4 5 6 7 8 9 10

MEALS

MEDICATIONS

Water Tracker

NOTES

....
....

DAY GOALS	
1	
2	
3	

DATE
WEEK
LOCATION
WEIGHT

Mood Tracker 😕 😐 😣 😢 😠 😃

BEHAVIOR

INATTENTION

SHORT ATTENTION	① ② ③ ④ ⑤ ⑥ ⑦ ⑧ ⑨ ⑩
UNMOTIVATED / BORED	① ② ③ ④ ⑤ ⑥ ⑦ ⑧ ⑨ ⑩
SHORT ATTENTION	① ② ③ ④ ⑤ ⑥ ⑦ ⑧ ⑨ ⑩
FORGETFUL / CONFUSIONED	① ② ③ ④ ⑤ ⑥ ⑦ ⑧ ⑨ ⑩

HYPERACTIVITY

CONSTANTLY MOVING / TALKING	① ② ③ ④ ⑤ ⑥ ⑦ ⑧ ⑨ ⑩
STRUGGLING TO SIT STILL	① ② ③ ④ ⑤ ⑥ ⑦ ⑧ ⑨ ⑩
TOUCHING THINGS REPEATEDLY	① ② ③ ④ ⑤ ⑥ ⑦ ⑧ ⑨ ⑩
DIFFICULT SLEEPING	① ② ③ ④ ⑤ ⑥ ⑦ ⑧ ⑨ ⑩

IMPULSIVITY

ACTING WITHOUT THINKING	① ② ③ ④ ⑤ ⑥ ⑦ ⑧ ⑨ ⑩
INTERRUPTING OTHERS	① ② ③ ④ ⑤ ⑥ ⑦ ⑧ ⑨ ⑩
EASILY FRUSTRATED	① ② ③ ④ ⑤ ⑥ ⑦ ⑧ ⑨ ⑩
UNABLE TO HOLD BACK EMOTIONS	① ② ③ ④ ⑤ ⑥ ⑦ ⑧ ⑨ ⑩

MEALS	MEDICATIONS

Water Tracker 🍼 🍼 🍼 🍼 🍼 🍼

NOTES

....
....

DAY GOALS	
1	
2	
3	

DATE
WEEK
LOCATION
WEIGHT

Mood Tracker 😟 😐 😖 😢 😠 😃

BEHAVIOR

INATTENTION

SHORT ATTENTION	① ② ③ ④ ⑤ ⑥ ⑦ ⑧ ⑨ ⑩
UNMOTIVATED / BORED	① ② ③ ④ ⑤ ⑥ ⑦ ⑧ ⑨ ⑩
SHORT ATTENTION	① ② ③ ④ ⑤ ⑥ ⑦ ⑧ ⑨ ⑩
FORGETFUL / CONFUSIONED	① ② ③ ④ ⑤ ⑥ ⑦ ⑧ ⑨ ⑩

HYPERACTIVITY

CONSTANTLY MOVING / TALKING	① ② ③ ④ ⑤ ⑥ ⑦ ⑧ ⑨ ⑩
STRUGGLING TO SIT STILL	① ② ③ ④ ⑤ ⑥ ⑦ ⑧ ⑨ ⑩
TOUCHING THINGS REPEATEDLY	① ② ③ ④ ⑤ ⑥ ⑦ ⑧ ⑨ ⑩
DIFFICULT SLEEPING	① ② ③ ④ ⑤ ⑥ ⑦ ⑧ ⑨ ⑩

IMPULSIVITY

ACTING WITHOUT THINKING	① ② ③ ④ ⑤ ⑥ ⑦ ⑧ ⑨ ⑩
INTERRUPTING OTHERS	① ② ③ ④ ⑤ ⑥ ⑦ ⑧ ⑨ ⑩
EASILY FRUSTRATED	① ② ③ ④ ⑤ ⑥ ⑦ ⑧ ⑨ ⑩
UNABLE TO HOLD BACK EMOTIONS	① ② ③ ④ ⑤ ⑥ ⑦ ⑧ ⑨ ⑩

MEALS	MEDICATIONS

Water Tracker 🍼 🍼 🍼 🍼 🍼 🍼 🍼

NOTES

....
....

DAY GOALS

1 ....
2 ....
3 ....

DATE
WEEK
LOCATION
WEIGHT

Mood Tracker

BEHAVIOR

INATTENTION

SHORT ATTENTION	① ② ③ ④ ⑤ ⑥ ⑦ ⑧ ⑨ ⑩
UNMOTIVATED / BORED	① ② ③ ④ ⑤ ⑥ ⑦ ⑧ ⑨ ⑩
SHORT ATTENTION	① ② ③ ④ ⑤ ⑥ ⑦ ⑧ ⑨ ⑩
FORGETFUL / CONFUSIONED	① ② ③ ④ ⑤ ⑥ ⑦ ⑧ ⑨ ⑩

HYPERACTIVITY

CONSTANTLY MOVING / TALKING	① ② ③ ④ ⑤ ⑥ ⑦ ⑧ ⑨ ⑩
STRUGGLING TO SIT STILL	① ② ③ ④ ⑤ ⑥ ⑦ ⑧ ⑨ ⑩
TOUCHING THINGS REPEATEDLY	① ② ③ ④ ⑤ ⑥ ⑦ ⑧ ⑨ ⑩
DIFFICULT SLEEPING	① ② ③ ④ ⑤ ⑥ ⑦ ⑧ ⑨ ⑩

IMPULSIVITY

ACTING WITHOUT THINKING	① ② ③ ④ ⑤ ⑥ ⑦ ⑧ ⑨ ⑩
INTERRUPTING OTHERS	① ② ③ ④ ⑤ ⑥ ⑦ ⑧ ⑨ ⑩
EASILY FRUSTRATED	① ② ③ ④ ⑤ ⑥ ⑦ ⑧ ⑨ ⑩
UNABLE TO HOLD BACK EMOTIONS	① ② ③ ④ ⑤ ⑥ ⑦ ⑧ ⑨ ⑩

MEALS

MEDICATIONS

Water Tracker

NOTES

....
....

DAY GOALS

1 ....
2 ....
3 ....

DATE
WEEK
LOCATION
WEIGHT

Mood Tracker

BEHAVIOR

INATTENTION

SHORT ATTENTION	① ② ③ ④ ⑤ ⑥ ⑦ ⑧ ⑨ ⑩
UNMOTIVATED / BORED	① ② ③ ④ ⑤ ⑥ ⑦ ⑧ ⑨ ⑩
SHORT ATTENTION	① ② ③ ④ ⑤ ⑥ ⑦ ⑧ ⑨ ⑩
FORGETFUL / CONFUSIONED	① ② ③ ④ ⑤ ⑥ ⑦ ⑧ ⑨ ⑩

HYPERACTIVITY

CONSTANTLY MOVING / TALKING	① ② ③ ④ ⑤ ⑥ ⑦ ⑧ ⑨ ⑩
STRUGGLING TO SIT STILL	① ② ③ ④ ⑤ ⑥ ⑦ ⑧ ⑨ ⑩
TOUCHING THINGS REPEATEDLY	① ② ③ ④ ⑤ ⑥ ⑦ ⑧ ⑨ ⑩
DIFFICULT SLEEPING	① ② ③ ④ ⑤ ⑥ ⑦ ⑧ ⑨ ⑩

IMPULSIVITY

ACTING WITHOUT THINKING	① ② ③ ④ ⑤ ⑥ ⑦ ⑧ ⑨ ⑩
INTERRUPTING OTHERS	① ② ③ ④ ⑤ ⑥ ⑦ ⑧ ⑨ ⑩
EASILY FRUSTRATED	① ② ③ ④ ⑤ ⑥ ⑦ ⑧ ⑨ ⑩
UNABLE TO HOLD BACK EMOTIONS	① ② ③ ④ ⑤ ⑥ ⑦ ⑧ ⑨ ⑩

MEALS

MEDICATIONS

Water Tracker

NOTES

....
....

DAY GOALS

1 ....
2 ....
3 ....

DATE
WEEK
LOCATION
WEIGHT

Mood Tracker ☹ 😐 😖 😢 😠 😃

BEHAVIOR

INATTENTION

Behavior	Rating
SHORT ATTENTION	① ② ③ ④ ⑤ ⑥ ⑦ ⑧ ⑨ ⑩
UNMOTIVATED / BORED	① ② ③ ④ ⑤ ⑥ ⑦ ⑧ ⑨ ⑩
SHORT ATTENTION	① ② ③ ④ ⑤ ⑥ ⑦ ⑧ ⑨ ⑩
FORGETFUL / CONFUSIONED	① ② ③ ④ ⑤ ⑥ ⑦ ⑧ ⑨ ⑩

HYPERACTIVITY

Behavior	Rating
CONSTANTLY MOVING / TALKING	① ② ③ ④ ⑤ ⑥ ⑦ ⑧ ⑨ ⑩
STRUGGLING TO SIT STILL	① ② ③ ④ ⑤ ⑥ ⑦ ⑧ ⑨ ⑩
TOUCHING THINGS REPEATEDLY	① ② ③ ④ ⑤ ⑥ ⑦ ⑧ ⑨ ⑩
DIFFICULT SLEEPING	① ② ③ ④ ⑤ ⑥ ⑦ ⑧ ⑨ ⑩

IMPULSIVITY

Behavior	Rating
ACTING WITHOUT THINKING	① ② ③ ④ ⑤ ⑥ ⑦ ⑧ ⑨ ⑩
INTERRUPTING OTHERS	① ② ③ ④ ⑤ ⑥ ⑦ ⑧ ⑨ ⑩
EASILY FRUSTRATED	① ② ③ ④ ⑤ ⑥ ⑦ ⑧ ⑨ ⑩
UNABLE TO HOLD BACK EMOTIONS	① ② ③ ④ ⑤ ⑥ ⑦ ⑧ ⑨ ⑩

MEALS

MEDICATIONS

Water Tracker 🍼 🍼 🍼 🍼 🍼 🍼 🍼

NOTES

....
....

DAY GOALS	
1	
2	
3	

DATE
WEEK
LOCATION
WEIGHT

Mood Tracker 😟 😐 😣 😢 😠 😃

BEHAVIOR

INATTENTION

SHORT ATTENTION	① ② ③ ④ ⑤ ⑥ ⑦ ⑧ ⑨ ⑩
UNMOTIVATED / BORED	① ② ③ ④ ⑤ ⑥ ⑦ ⑧ ⑨ ⑩
SHORT ATTENTION	① ② ③ ④ ⑤ ⑥ ⑦ ⑧ ⑨ ⑩
FORGETFUL / CONFUSIONED	① ② ③ ④ ⑤ ⑥ ⑦ ⑧ ⑨ ⑩

HYPERACTIVITY

CONSTANTLY MOVING / TALKING	① ② ③ ④ ⑤ ⑥ ⑦ ⑧ ⑨ ⑩
STRUGGLING TO SIT STILL	① ② ③ ④ ⑤ ⑥ ⑦ ⑧ ⑨ ⑩
TOUCHING THINGS REPEATEDLY	① ② ③ ④ ⑤ ⑥ ⑦ ⑧ ⑨ ⑩
DIFFICULT SLEEPING	① ② ③ ④ ⑤ ⑥ ⑦ ⑧ ⑨ ⑩

IMPULSIVITY

ACTING WITHOUT THINKING	① ② ③ ④ ⑤ ⑥ ⑦ ⑧ ⑨ ⑩
INTERRUPTING OTHERS	① ② ③ ④ ⑤ ⑥ ⑦ ⑧ ⑨ ⑩
EASILY FRUSTRATED	① ② ③ ④ ⑤ ⑥ ⑦ ⑧ ⑨ ⑩
UNABLE TO HOLD BACK EMOTIONS	① ② ③ ④ ⑤ ⑥ ⑦ ⑧ ⑨ ⑩

MEALS	MEDICATIONS

Water Tracker 🍼 🍼 🍼 🍼 🍼 🍼 🍼

NOTES

....
....

DAY GOALS

1 ....
2 ....
3 ....

DATE ....
WEEK ....
LOCATION ....
WEIGHT ....

Mood Tracker 😕 😐 😖 😢 😠 😃

BEHAVIOR

INATTENTION

SHORT ATTENTION	① ② ③ ④ ⑤ ⑥ ⑦ ⑧ ⑨ ⑩
UNMOTIVATED / BORED	① ② ③ ④ ⑤ ⑥ ⑦ ⑧ ⑨ ⑩
SHORT ATTENTION	① ② ③ ④ ⑤ ⑥ ⑦ ⑧ ⑨ ⑩
FORGETFUL / CONFUSIONED	① ② ③ ④ ⑤ ⑥ ⑦ ⑧ ⑨ ⑩

HYPERACTIVITY

CONSTANTLY MOVING / TALKING	① ② ③ ④ ⑤ ⑥ ⑦ ⑧ ⑨ ⑩
STRUGGLING TO SIT STILL	① ② ③ ④ ⑤ ⑥ ⑦ ⑧ ⑨ ⑩
TOUCHING THINGS REPEATEDLY	① ② ③ ④ ⑤ ⑥ ⑦ ⑧ ⑨ ⑩
DIFFICULT SLEEPING	① ② ③ ④ ⑤ ⑥ ⑦ ⑧ ⑨ ⑩

IMPULSIVITY

ACTING WITHOUT THINKING	① ② ③ ④ ⑤ ⑥ ⑦ ⑧ ⑨ ⑩
INTERRUPTING OTHERS	① ② ③ ④ ⑤ ⑥ ⑦ ⑧ ⑨ ⑩
EASILY FRUSTRATED	① ② ③ ④ ⑤ ⑥ ⑦ ⑧ ⑨ ⑩
UNABLE TO HOLD BACK EMOTIONS	① ② ③ ④ ⑤ ⑥ ⑦ ⑧ ⑨ ⑩

MEALS

MEDICATIONS

Water Tracker 🍼 🍼 🍼 🍼 🍼 🍼

NOTES

....
....

DAY GOALS

1 ....
2 ....
3 ....

DATE
WEEK
LOCATION
WEIGHT

Mood Tracker 😟 😐 😖 😢 😠 😃

BEHAVIOR

INATTENTION

SHORT ATTENTION	① ② ③ ④ ⑤ ⑥ ⑦ ⑧ ⑨ ⑩
UNMOTIVATED / BORED	① ② ③ ④ ⑤ ⑥ ⑦ ⑧ ⑨ ⑩
SHORT ATTENTION	① ② ③ ④ ⑤ ⑥ ⑦ ⑧ ⑨ ⑩
FORGETFUL / CONFUSIONED	① ② ③ ④ ⑤ ⑥ ⑦ ⑧ ⑨ ⑩

HYPERACTIVITY

CONSTANTLY MOVING / TALKING	① ② ③ ④ ⑤ ⑥ ⑦ ⑧ ⑨ ⑩
STRUGGLING TO SIT STILL	① ② ③ ④ ⑤ ⑥ ⑦ ⑧ ⑨ ⑩
TOUCHING THINGS REPEATEDLY	① ② ③ ④ ⑤ ⑥ ⑦ ⑧ ⑨ ⑩
DIFFICULT SLEEPING	① ② ③ ④ ⑤ ⑥ ⑦ ⑧ ⑨ ⑩

IMPULSIVITY

ACTING WITHOUT THINKING	① ② ③ ④ ⑤ ⑥ ⑦ ⑧ ⑨ ⑩
INTERRUPTING OTHERS	① ② ③ ④ ⑤ ⑥ ⑦ ⑧ ⑨ ⑩
EASILY FRUSTRATED	① ② ③ ④ ⑤ ⑥ ⑦ ⑧ ⑨ ⑩
UNABLE TO HOLD BACK EMOTIONS	① ② ③ ④ ⑤ ⑥ ⑦ ⑧ ⑨ ⑩

MEALS

MEDICATIONS

Water Tracker 🍼 🍼 🍼 🍼 🍼 🍼 🍼

NOTES

....
....

DAY GOALS	
1	
2	
3	

DATE
WEEK
LOCATION
WEIGHT

Mood Tracker

BEHAVIOR

INATTENTION

SHORT ATTENTION	① ② ③ ④ ⑤ ⑥ ⑦ ⑧ ⑨ ⑩
UNMOTIVATED / BORED	① ② ③ ④ ⑤ ⑥ ⑦ ⑧ ⑨ ⑩
SHORT ATTENTION	① ② ③ ④ ⑤ ⑥ ⑦ ⑧ ⑨ ⑩
FORGETFUL / CONFUSIONED	① ② ③ ④ ⑤ ⑥ ⑦ ⑧ ⑨ ⑩

HYPERACTIVITY

CONSTANTLY MOVING / TALKING	① ② ③ ④ ⑤ ⑥ ⑦ ⑧ ⑨ ⑩
STRUGGLING TO SIT STILL	① ② ③ ④ ⑤ ⑥ ⑦ ⑧ ⑨ ⑩
TOUCHING THINGS REPEATEDLY	① ② ③ ④ ⑤ ⑥ ⑦ ⑧ ⑨ ⑩
DIFFICULT SLEEPING	① ② ③ ④ ⑤ ⑥ ⑦ ⑧ ⑨ ⑩

IMPULSIVITY

ACTING WITHOUT THINKING	① ② ③ ④ ⑤ ⑥ ⑦ ⑧ ⑨ ⑩
INTERRUPTING OTHERS	① ② ③ ④ ⑤ ⑥ ⑦ ⑧ ⑨ ⑩
EASILY FRUSTRATED	① ② ③ ④ ⑤ ⑥ ⑦ ⑧ ⑨ ⑩
UNABLE TO HOLD BACK EMOTIONS	① ② ③ ④ ⑤ ⑥ ⑦ ⑧ ⑨ ⑩

MEALS	MEDICATIONS

Water Tracker

NOTES

....
....

DAY GOALS	
1	DATE
2	WEEK
3	LOCATION
	WEIGHT

Mood Tracker 😕 😐 😖 😢 😠 😃

BEHAVIOR

INATTENTION

SHORT ATTENTION	① ② ③ ④ ⑤ ⑥ ⑦ ⑧ ⑨ ⑩
UNMOTIVATED / BORED	① ② ③ ④ ⑤ ⑥ ⑦ ⑧ ⑨ ⑩
SHORT ATTENTION	① ② ③ ④ ⑤ ⑥ ⑦ ⑧ ⑨ ⑩
FORGETFUL / CONFUSIONED	① ② ③ ④ ⑤ ⑥ ⑦ ⑧ ⑨ ⑩

HYPERACTIVITY

CONSTANTLY MOVING / TALKING	① ② ③ ④ ⑤ ⑥ ⑦ ⑧ ⑨ ⑩
STRUGGLING TO SIT STILL	① ② ③ ④ ⑤ ⑥ ⑦ ⑧ ⑨ ⑩
TOUCHING THINGS REPEATEDLY	① ② ③ ④ ⑤ ⑥ ⑦ ⑧ ⑨ ⑩
DIFFICULT SLEEPING	① ② ③ ④ ⑤ ⑥ ⑦ ⑧ ⑨ ⑩

IMPULSIVITY

ACTING WITHOUT THINKING	① ② ③ ④ ⑤ ⑥ ⑦ ⑧ ⑨ ⑩
INTERRUPTING OTHERS	① ② ③ ④ ⑤ ⑥ ⑦ ⑧ ⑨ ⑩
EASILY FRUSTRATED	① ② ③ ④ ⑤ ⑥ ⑦ ⑧ ⑨ ⑩
UNABLE TO HOLD BACK EMOTIONS	① ② ③ ④ ⑤ ⑥ ⑦ ⑧ ⑨ ⑩

MEALS	MEDICATIONS

Water Tracker 🍼 🍼 🍼 🍼 🍼 🍼 🍼

NOTES

....
....

DAY GOALS	
1	DATE
2	WEEK
3	LOCATION
	WEIGHT

Mood Tracker 😕 😐 😖 😢 😠 😃

BEHAVIOR

INATTENTION

SHORT ATTENTION	① ② ③ ④ ⑤ ⑥ ⑦ ⑧ ⑨ ⑩
UNMOTIVATED / BORED	① ② ③ ④ ⑤ ⑥ ⑦ ⑧ ⑨ ⑩
SHORT ATTENTION	① ② ③ ④ ⑤ ⑥ ⑦ ⑧ ⑨ ⑩
FORGETFUL / CONFUSIONED	① ② ③ ④ ⑤ ⑥ ⑦ ⑧ ⑨ ⑩

HYPERACTIVITY

CONSTANTLY MOVING / TALKING	① ② ③ ④ ⑤ ⑥ ⑦ ⑧ ⑨ ⑩
STRUGGLING TO SIT STILL	① ② ③ ④ ⑤ ⑥ ⑦ ⑧ ⑨ ⑩
TOUCHING THINGS REPEATEDLY	① ② ③ ④ ⑤ ⑥ ⑦ ⑧ ⑨ ⑩
DIFFICULT SLEEPING	① ② ③ ④ ⑤ ⑥ ⑦ ⑧ ⑨ ⑩

IMPULSIVITY

ACTING WITHOUT THINKING	① ② ③ ④ ⑤ ⑥ ⑦ ⑧ ⑨ ⑩
INTERRUPTING OTHERS	① ② ③ ④ ⑤ ⑥ ⑦ ⑧ ⑨ ⑩
EASILY FRUSTRATED	① ② ③ ④ ⑤ ⑥ ⑦ ⑧ ⑨ ⑩
UNABLE TO HOLD BACK EMOTIONS	① ② ③ ④ ⑤ ⑥ ⑦ ⑧ ⑨ ⑩

MEALS	MEDICATIONS

Water Tracker 🍼 🍼 🍼 🍼 🍼 🍼 🍼

NOTES

....
....

DAY GOALS

1 ....
2 ....
3 ....

DATE
WEEK
LOCATION
WEIGHT

Mood Tracker

BEHAVIOR

INATTENTION

SHORT ATTENTION	① ② ③ ④ ⑤ ⑥ ⑦ ⑧ ⑨ ⑩
UNMOTIVATED / BORED	① ② ③ ④ ⑤ ⑥ ⑦ ⑧ ⑨ ⑩
SHORT ATTENTION	① ② ③ ④ ⑤ ⑥ ⑦ ⑧ ⑨ ⑩
FORGETFUL / CONFUSIONED	① ② ③ ④ ⑤ ⑥ ⑦ ⑧ ⑨ ⑩

HYPERACTIVITY

CONSTANTLY MOVING / TALKING	① ② ③ ④ ⑤ ⑥ ⑦ ⑧ ⑨ ⑩
STRUGGLING TO SIT STILL	① ② ③ ④ ⑤ ⑥ ⑦ ⑧ ⑨ ⑩
TOUCHING THINGS REPEATEDLY	① ② ③ ④ ⑤ ⑥ ⑦ ⑧ ⑨ ⑩
DIFFICULT SLEEPING	① ② ③ ④ ⑤ ⑥ ⑦ ⑧ ⑨ ⑩

IMPULSIVITY

ACTING WITHOUT THINKING	① ② ③ ④ ⑤ ⑥ ⑦ ⑧ ⑨ ⑩
INTERRUPTING OTHERS	① ② ③ ④ ⑤ ⑥ ⑦ ⑧ ⑨ ⑩
EASILY FRUSTRATED	① ② ③ ④ ⑤ ⑥ ⑦ ⑧ ⑨ ⑩
UNABLE TO HOLD BACK EMOTIONS	① ② ③ ④ ⑤ ⑥ ⑦ ⑧ ⑨ ⑩

MEALS

MEDICATIONS

Water Tracker

NOTES

....
....

DAY GOALS

1 ....
2 ....
3 ....

DATE ....
WEEK ....
LOCATION ....
WEIGHT ....

Mood Tracker 😕 😐 😣 😢 😠 😀

BEHAVIOR

INATTENTION

SHORT ATTENTION	① ② ③ ④ ⑤ ⑥ ⑦ ⑧ ⑨ ⑩
UNMOTIVATED / BORED	① ② ③ ④ ⑤ ⑥ ⑦ ⑧ ⑨ ⑩
SHORT ATTENTION	① ② ③ ④ ⑤ ⑥ ⑦ ⑧ ⑨ ⑩
FORGETFUL / CONFUSIONED	① ② ③ ④ ⑤ ⑥ ⑦ ⑧ ⑨ ⑩

HYPERACTIVITY

CONSTANTLY MOVING / TALKING	① ② ③ ④ ⑤ ⑥ ⑦ ⑧ ⑨ ⑩
STRUGGLING TO SIT STILL	① ② ③ ④ ⑤ ⑥ ⑦ ⑧ ⑨ ⑩
TOUCHING THINGS REPEATEDLY	① ② ③ ④ ⑤ ⑥ ⑦ ⑧ ⑨ ⑩
DIFFICULT SLEEPING	① ② ③ ④ ⑤ ⑥ ⑦ ⑧ ⑨ ⑩

IMPULSIVITY

ACTING WITHOUT THINKING	① ② ③ ④ ⑤ ⑥ ⑦ ⑧ ⑨ ⑩
INTERRUPTING OTHERS	① ② ③ ④ ⑤ ⑥ ⑦ ⑧ ⑨ ⑩
EASILY FRUSTRATED	① ② ③ ④ ⑤ ⑥ ⑦ ⑧ ⑨ ⑩
UNABLE TO HOLD BACK EMOTIONS	① ② ③ ④ ⑤ ⑥ ⑦ ⑧ ⑨ ⑩

MEALS

MEDICATIONS

Water Tracker 🍼 🍼 🍼 🍼 🍼 🍼 🍼

NOTES

....
....

DAY GOALS

1 ....
2 ....
3 ....

DATE
WEEK
LOCATION
WEIGHT

Mood Tracker

BEHAVIOR

INATTENTION

SHORT ATTENTION	① ② ③ ④ ⑤ ⑥ ⑦ ⑧ ⑨ ⑩
UNMOTIVATED / BORED	① ② ③ ④ ⑤ ⑥ ⑦ ⑧ ⑨ ⑩
SHORT ATTENTION	① ② ③ ④ ⑤ ⑥ ⑦ ⑧ ⑨ ⑩
FORGETFUL / CONFUSIONED	① ② ③ ④ ⑤ ⑥ ⑦ ⑧ ⑨ ⑩

HYPERACTIVITY

CONSTANTLY MOVING / TALKING	① ② ③ ④ ⑤ ⑥ ⑦ ⑧ ⑨ ⑩
STRUGGLING TO SIT STILL	① ② ③ ④ ⑤ ⑥ ⑦ ⑧ ⑨ ⑩
TOUCHING THINGS REPEATEDLY	① ② ③ ④ ⑤ ⑥ ⑦ ⑧ ⑨ ⑩
DIFFICULT SLEEPING	① ② ③ ④ ⑤ ⑥ ⑦ ⑧ ⑨ ⑩

IMPULSIVITY

ACTING WITHOUT THINKING	① ② ③ ④ ⑤ ⑥ ⑦ ⑧ ⑨ ⑩
INTERRUPTING OTHERS	① ② ③ ④ ⑤ ⑥ ⑦ ⑧ ⑨ ⑩
EASILY FRUSTRATED	① ② ③ ④ ⑤ ⑥ ⑦ ⑧ ⑨ ⑩
UNABLE TO HOLD BACK EMOTIONS	① ② ③ ④ ⑤ ⑥ ⑦ ⑧ ⑨ ⑩

MEALS

MEDICATIONS

Water Tracker

NOTES

DAY GOALS	
1	
2	
3	

DATE
WEEK
LOCATION
WEIGHT

Mood Tracker   😕 😐 😖 😢 😠 😃

BEHAVIOR

INATTENTION

SHORT ATTENTION	① ② ③ ④ ⑤ ⑥ ⑦ ⑧ ⑨ ⑩
UNMOTIVATED / BORED	① ② ③ ④ ⑤ ⑥ ⑦ ⑧ ⑨ ⑩
SHORT ATTENTION	① ② ③ ④ ⑤ ⑥ ⑦ ⑧ ⑨ ⑩
FORGETFUL / CONFUSIONED	① ② ③ ④ ⑤ ⑥ ⑦ ⑧ ⑨ ⑩

HYPERACTIVITY

CONSTANTLY MOVING / TALKING	① ② ③ ④ ⑤ ⑥ ⑦ ⑧ ⑨ ⑩
STRUGGLING TO SIT STILL	① ② ③ ④ ⑤ ⑥ ⑦ ⑧ ⑨ ⑩
TOUCHING THINGS REPEATEDLY	① ② ③ ④ ⑤ ⑥ ⑦ ⑧ ⑨ ⑩
DIFFICULT SLEEPING	① ② ③ ④ ⑤ ⑥ ⑦ ⑧ ⑨ ⑩

IMPULSIVITY

ACTING WITHOUT THINKING	① ② ③ ④ ⑤ ⑥ ⑦ ⑧ ⑨ ⑩
INTERRUPTING OTHERS	① ② ③ ④ ⑤ ⑥ ⑦ ⑧ ⑨ ⑩
EASILY FRUSTRATED	① ② ③ ④ ⑤ ⑥ ⑦ ⑧ ⑨ ⑩
UNABLE TO HOLD BACK EMOTIONS	① ② ③ ④ ⑤ ⑥ ⑦ ⑧ ⑨ ⑩

MEALS	MEDICATIONS

Water Tracker 🍶 🍶 🍶 🍶 🍶 🍶 🍶 🍶

NOTES

....
....

DAY GOALS

1 ....
2 ....
3 ....

DATE
WEEK
LOCATION
WEIGHT

Mood Tracker 😟 😐 😖 😢 😠 😃

BEHAVIOR

INATTENTION

Behavior	Rating
SHORT ATTENTION	① ② ③ ④ ⑤ ⑥ ⑦ ⑧ ⑨ ⑩
UNMOTIVATED / BORED	① ② ③ ④ ⑤ ⑥ ⑦ ⑧ ⑨ ⑩
SHORT ATTENTION	① ② ③ ④ ⑤ ⑥ ⑦ ⑧ ⑨ ⑩
FORGETFUL / CONFUSIONED	① ② ③ ④ ⑤ ⑥ ⑦ ⑧ ⑨ ⑩

HYPERACTIVITY

Behavior	Rating
CONSTANTLY MOVING / TALKING	① ② ③ ④ ⑤ ⑥ ⑦ ⑧ ⑨ ⑩
STRUGGLING TO SIT STILL	① ② ③ ④ ⑤ ⑥ ⑦ ⑧ ⑨ ⑩
TOUCHING THINGS REPEATEDLY	① ② ③ ④ ⑤ ⑥ ⑦ ⑧ ⑨ ⑩
DIFFICULT SLEEPING	① ② ③ ④ ⑤ ⑥ ⑦ ⑧ ⑨ ⑩

IMPULSIVITY

Behavior	Rating
ACTING WITHOUT THINKING	① ② ③ ④ ⑤ ⑥ ⑦ ⑧ ⑨ ⑩
INTERRUPTING OTHERS	① ② ③ ④ ⑤ ⑥ ⑦ ⑧ ⑨ ⑩
EASILY FRUSTRATED	① ② ③ ④ ⑤ ⑥ ⑦ ⑧ ⑨ ⑩
UNABLE TO HOLD BACK EMOTIONS	① ② ③ ④ ⑤ ⑥ ⑦ ⑧ ⑨ ⑩

MEALS	MEDICATIONS

Water Tracker 🍶 🍶 🍶 🍶 🍶 🍶 🍶 🍶

NOTES

....
....

DAY GOALS	
1	
2	
3	

DATE
WEEK
LOCATION
WEIGHT

Mood Tracker

BEHAVIOR

INATTENTION

SHORT ATTENTION	① ② ③ ④ ⑤ ⑥ ⑦ ⑧ ⑨ ⑩
UNMOTIVATED / BORED	① ② ③ ④ ⑤ ⑥ ⑦ ⑧ ⑨ ⑩
SHORT ATTENTION	① ② ③ ④ ⑤ ⑥ ⑦ ⑧ ⑨ ⑩
FORGETFUL / CONFUSIONED	① ② ③ ④ ⑤ ⑥ ⑦ ⑧ ⑨ ⑩

HYPERACTIVITY

CONSTANTLY MOVING / TALKING	① ② ③ ④ ⑤ ⑥ ⑦ ⑧ ⑨ ⑩
STRUGGLING TO SIT STILL	① ② ③ ④ ⑤ ⑥ ⑦ ⑧ ⑨ ⑩
TOUCHING THINGS REPEATEDLY	① ② ③ ④ ⑤ ⑥ ⑦ ⑧ ⑨ ⑩
DIFFICULT SLEEPING	① ② ③ ④ ⑤ ⑥ ⑦ ⑧ ⑨ ⑩

IMPULSIVITY

ACTING WITHOUT THINKING	① ② ③ ④ ⑤ ⑥ ⑦ ⑧ ⑨ ⑩
INTERRUPTING OTHERS	① ② ③ ④ ⑤ ⑥ ⑦ ⑧ ⑨ ⑩
EASILY FRUSTRATED	① ② ③ ④ ⑤ ⑥ ⑦ ⑧ ⑨ ⑩
UNABLE TO HOLD BACK EMOTIONS	① ② ③ ④ ⑤ ⑥ ⑦ ⑧ ⑨ ⑩

MEALS	MEDICATIONS

Water Tracker

NOTES

....
....

DAY GOALS	
1	DATE
2	WEEK
3	LOCATION
	WEIGHT

Mood Tracker 😕 😐 😖 😢 😠 😃

BEHAVIOR

INATTENTION

SHORT ATTENTION	① ② ③ ④ ⑤ ⑥ ⑦ ⑧ ⑨ ⑩
UNMOTIVATED / BORED	① ② ③ ④ ⑤ ⑥ ⑦ ⑧ ⑨ ⑩
SHORT ATTENTION	① ② ③ ④ ⑤ ⑥ ⑦ ⑧ ⑨ ⑩
FORGETFUL / CONFUSIONED	① ② ③ ④ ⑤ ⑥ ⑦ ⑧ ⑨ ⑩

HYPERACTIVITY

CONSTANTLY MOVING / TALKING	① ② ③ ④ ⑤ ⑥ ⑦ ⑧ ⑨ ⑩
STRUGGLING TO SIT STILL	① ② ③ ④ ⑤ ⑥ ⑦ ⑧ ⑨ ⑩
TOUCHING THINGS REPEATEDLY	① ② ③ ④ ⑤ ⑥ ⑦ ⑧ ⑨ ⑩
DIFFICULT SLEEPING	① ② ③ ④ ⑤ ⑥ ⑦ ⑧ ⑨ ⑩

IMPULSIVITY

ACTING WITHOUT THINKING	① ② ③ ④ ⑤ ⑥ ⑦ ⑧ ⑨ ⑩
INTERRUPTING OTHERS	① ② ③ ④ ⑤ ⑥ ⑦ ⑧ ⑨ ⑩
EASILY FRUSTRATED	① ② ③ ④ ⑤ ⑥ ⑦ ⑧ ⑨ ⑩
UNABLE TO HOLD BACK EMOTIONS	① ② ③ ④ ⑤ ⑥ ⑦ ⑧ ⑨ ⑩

MEALS	MEDICATIONS

Water Tracker 🍼 🍼 🍼 🍼 🍼 🍼 🍼

NOTES

....
....

DAY GOALS	
1	
2	
3	

DATE
WEEK
LOCATION
WEIGHT

Mood Tracker 🙁 😐 😖 😢 😠 😃

BEHAVIOR

INATTENTION

SHORT ATTENTION	① ② ③ ④ ⑤ ⑥ ⑦ ⑧ ⑨ ⑩
UNMOTIVATED / BORED	① ② ③ ④ ⑤ ⑥ ⑦ ⑧ ⑨ ⑩
SHORT ATTENTION	① ② ③ ④ ⑤ ⑥ ⑦ ⑧ ⑨ ⑩
FORGETFUL / CONFUSIONED	① ② ③ ④ ⑤ ⑥ ⑦ ⑧ ⑨ ⑩

HYPERACTIVITY

CONSTANTLY MOVING / TALKING	① ② ③ ④ ⑤ ⑥ ⑦ ⑧ ⑨ ⑩
STRUGGLING TO SIT STILL	① ② ③ ④ ⑤ ⑥ ⑦ ⑧ ⑨ ⑩
TOUCHING THINGS REPEATEDLY	① ② ③ ④ ⑤ ⑥ ⑦ ⑧ ⑨ ⑩
DIFFICULT SLEEPING	① ② ③ ④ ⑤ ⑥ ⑦ ⑧ ⑨ ⑩

IMPULSIVITY

ACTING WITHOUT THINKING	① ② ③ ④ ⑤ ⑥ ⑦ ⑧ ⑨ ⑩
INTERRUPTING OTHERS	① ② ③ ④ ⑤ ⑥ ⑦ ⑧ ⑨ ⑩
EASILY FRUSTRATED	① ② ③ ④ ⑤ ⑥ ⑦ ⑧ ⑨ ⑩
UNABLE TO HOLD BACK EMOTIONS	① ② ③ ④ ⑤ ⑥ ⑦ ⑧ ⑨ ⑩

MEALS	MEDICATIONS

Water Tracker 🍼 🍼 🍼 🍼 🍼 🍼 🍼

NOTES

....
....

DAY GOALS

1 ....
2 ....
3 ....

DATE
WEEK
LOCATION
WEIGHT

Mood Tracker

BEHAVIOR

INATTENTION

SHORT ATTENTION	① ② ③ ④ ⑤ ⑥ ⑦ ⑧ ⑨ ⑩
UNMOTIVATED / BORED	① ② ③ ④ ⑤ ⑥ ⑦ ⑧ ⑨ ⑩
SHORT ATTENTION	① ② ③ ④ ⑤ ⑥ ⑦ ⑧ ⑨ ⑩
FORGETFUL / CONFUSIONED	① ② ③ ④ ⑤ ⑥ ⑦ ⑧ ⑨ ⑩

HYPERACTIVITY

CONSTANTLY MOVING / TALKING	① ② ③ ④ ⑤ ⑥ ⑦ ⑧ ⑨ ⑩
STRUGGLING TO SIT STILL	① ② ③ ④ ⑤ ⑥ ⑦ ⑧ ⑨ ⑩
TOUCHING THINGS REPEATEDLY	① ② ③ ④ ⑤ ⑥ ⑦ ⑧ ⑨ ⑩
DIFFICULT SLEEPING	① ② ③ ④ ⑤ ⑥ ⑦ ⑧ ⑨ ⑩

IMPULSIVITY

ACTING WITHOUT THINKING	① ② ③ ④ ⑤ ⑥ ⑦ ⑧ ⑨ ⑩
INTERRUPTING OTHERS	① ② ③ ④ ⑤ ⑥ ⑦ ⑧ ⑨ ⑩
EASILY FRUSTRATED	① ② ③ ④ ⑤ ⑥ ⑦ ⑧ ⑨ ⑩
UNABLE TO HOLD BACK EMOTIONS	① ② ③ ④ ⑤ ⑥ ⑦ ⑧ ⑨ ⑩

MEALS

MEDICATIONS

Water Tracker

NOTES

....
....

DAY GOALS

1 ....
2 ....
3 ....

DATE
WEEK
LOCATION
WEIGHT

Mood Tracker 🙂 😐 😖 😢 😠 😃

BEHAVIOR

INATTENTION

SHORT ATTENTION	① ② ③ ④ ⑤ ⑥ ⑦ ⑧ ⑨ ⑩
UNMOTIVATED / BORED	① ② ③ ④ ⑤ ⑥ ⑦ ⑧ ⑨ ⑩
SHORT ATTENTION	① ② ③ ④ ⑤ ⑥ ⑦ ⑧ ⑨ ⑩
FORGETFUL / CONFUSIONED	① ② ③ ④ ⑤ ⑥ ⑦ ⑧ ⑨ ⑩

HYPERACTIVITY

CONSTANTLY MOVING / TALKING	① ② ③ ④ ⑤ ⑥ ⑦ ⑧ ⑨ ⑩
STRUGGLING TO SIT STILL	① ② ③ ④ ⑤ ⑥ ⑦ ⑧ ⑨ ⑩
TOUCHING THINGS REPEATEDLY	① ② ③ ④ ⑤ ⑥ ⑦ ⑧ ⑨ ⑩
DIFFICULT SLEEPING	① ② ③ ④ ⑤ ⑥ ⑦ ⑧ ⑨ ⑩

IMPULSIVITY

ACTING WITHOUT THINKING	① ② ③ ④ ⑤ ⑥ ⑦ ⑧ ⑨ ⑩
INTERRUPTING OTHERS	① ② ③ ④ ⑤ ⑥ ⑦ ⑧ ⑨ ⑩
EASILY FRUSTRATED	① ② ③ ④ ⑤ ⑥ ⑦ ⑧ ⑨ ⑩
UNABLE TO HOLD BACK EMOTIONS	① ② ③ ④ ⑤ ⑥ ⑦ ⑧ ⑨ ⑩

MEALS

MEDICATIONS

Water Tracker 🍼 🍼 🍼 🍼 🍼 🍼 🍼

NOTES

....
....

DAY GOALS

1 ....
2 ....
3 ....

DATE
WEEK
LOCATION
WEIGHT

Mood Tracker 😞 😐 😖 😢 😠 😃

BEHAVIOR

INATTENTION

SHORT ATTENTION	① ② ③ ④ ⑤ ⑥ ⑦ ⑧ ⑨ ⑩
UNMOTIVATED / BORED	① ② ③ ④ ⑤ ⑥ ⑦ ⑧ ⑨ ⑩
SHORT ATTENTION	① ② ③ ④ ⑤ ⑥ ⑦ ⑧ ⑨ ⑩
FORGETFUL / CONFUSIONED	① ② ③ ④ ⑤ ⑥ ⑦ ⑧ ⑨ ⑩

HYPERACTIVITY

CONSTANTLY MOVING / TALKING	① ② ③ ④ ⑤ ⑥ ⑦ ⑧ ⑨ ⑩
STRUGGLING TO SIT STILL	① ② ③ ④ ⑤ ⑥ ⑦ ⑧ ⑨ ⑩
TOUCHING THINGS REPEATEDLY	① ② ③ ④ ⑤ ⑥ ⑦ ⑧ ⑨ ⑩
DIFFICULT SLEEPING	① ② ③ ④ ⑤ ⑥ ⑦ ⑧ ⑨ ⑩

IMPULSIVITY

ACTING WITHOUT THINKING	① ② ③ ④ ⑤ ⑥ ⑦ ⑧ ⑨ ⑩
INTERRUPTING OTHERS	① ② ③ ④ ⑤ ⑥ ⑦ ⑧ ⑨ ⑩
EASILY FRUSTRATED	① ② ③ ④ ⑤ ⑥ ⑦ ⑧ ⑨ ⑩
UNABLE TO HOLD BACK EMOTIONS	① ② ③ ④ ⑤ ⑥ ⑦ ⑧ ⑨ ⑩

MEALS

MEDICATIONS

Water Tracker 🍼 🍼 🍼 🍼 🍼 🍼 🍼

NOTES

....
....

DAY GOALS	
1	
2	
3	

DATE
WEEK
LOCATION
WEIGHT

Mood Tracker 😕 😐 😖 😢 😠 😃

BEHAVIOR

INATTENTION

SHORT ATTENTION	① ② ③ ④ ⑤ ⑥ ⑦ ⑧ ⑨ ⑩
UNMOTIVATED / BORED	① ② ③ ④ ⑤ ⑥ ⑦ ⑧ ⑨ ⑩
SHORT ATTENTION	① ② ③ ④ ⑤ ⑥ ⑦ ⑧ ⑨ ⑩
FORGETFUL / CONFUSIONED	① ② ③ ④ ⑤ ⑥ ⑦ ⑧ ⑨ ⑩

HYPERACTIVITY

CONSTANTLY MOVING / TALKING	① ② ③ ④ ⑤ ⑥ ⑦ ⑧ ⑨ ⑩
STRUGGLING TO SIT STILL	① ② ③ ④ ⑤ ⑥ ⑦ ⑧ ⑨ ⑩
TOUCHING THINGS REPEATEDLY	① ② ③ ④ ⑤ ⑥ ⑦ ⑧ ⑨ ⑩
DIFFICULT SLEEPING	① ② ③ ④ ⑤ ⑥ ⑦ ⑧ ⑨ ⑩

IMPULSIVITY

ACTING WITHOUT THINKING	① ② ③ ④ ⑤ ⑥ ⑦ ⑧ ⑨ ⑩
INTERRUPTING OTHERS	① ② ③ ④ ⑤ ⑥ ⑦ ⑧ ⑨ ⑩
EASILY FRUSTRATED	① ② ③ ④ ⑤ ⑥ ⑦ ⑧ ⑨ ⑩
UNABLE TO HOLD BACK EMOTIONS	① ② ③ ④ ⑤ ⑥ ⑦ ⑧ ⑨ ⑩

MEALS	MEDICATIONS

Water Tracker 🍼 🍼 🍼 🍼 🍼 🍼 🍼

NOTES

....
....

DAY GOALS
1 ....
2 ....
3 ....

DATE
WEEK
LOCATION
WEIGHT

Mood Tracker 😕 😐 😖 😢 😠 😃

BEHAVIOR

INATTENTION

SHORT ATTENTION	① ② ③ ④ ⑤ ⑥ ⑦ ⑧ ⑨ ⑩
UNMOTIVATED / BORED	① ② ③ ④ ⑤ ⑥ ⑦ ⑧ ⑨ ⑩
SHORT ATTENTION	① ② ③ ④ ⑤ ⑥ ⑦ ⑧ ⑨ ⑩
FORGETFUL / CONFUSIONED	① ② ③ ④ ⑤ ⑥ ⑦ ⑧ ⑨ ⑩

HYPERACTIVITY

CONSTANTLY MOVING / TALKING	① ② ③ ④ ⑤ ⑥ ⑦ ⑧ ⑨ ⑩
STRUGGLING TO SIT STILL	① ② ③ ④ ⑤ ⑥ ⑦ ⑧ ⑨ ⑩
TOUCHING THINGS REPEATEDLY	① ② ③ ④ ⑤ ⑥ ⑦ ⑧ ⑨ ⑩
DIFFICULT SLEEPING	① ② ③ ④ ⑤ ⑥ ⑦ ⑧ ⑨ ⑩

IMPULSIVITY

ACTING WITHOUT THINKING	① ② ③ ④ ⑤ ⑥ ⑦ ⑧ ⑨ ⑩
INTERRUPTING OTHERS	① ② ③ ④ ⑤ ⑥ ⑦ ⑧ ⑨ ⑩
EASILY FRUSTRATED	① ② ③ ④ ⑤ ⑥ ⑦ ⑧ ⑨ ⑩
UNABLE TO HOLD BACK EMOTIONS	① ② ③ ④ ⑤ ⑥ ⑦ ⑧ ⑨ ⑩

MEALS	MEDICATIONS

Water Tracker 🍼 🍼 🍼 🍼 🍼 🍼 🍼

NOTES

....
....

DAY GOALS

1 ....
2 ....
3 ....

DATE
WEEK
LOCATION
WEIGHT

Mood Tracker 😟 😐 😖 😢 😠 😃

BEHAVIOR

INATTENTION

SHORT ATTENTION	① ② ③ ④ ⑤ ⑥ ⑦ ⑧ ⑨ ⑩
UNMOTIVATED / BORED	① ② ③ ④ ⑤ ⑥ ⑦ ⑧ ⑨ ⑩
SHORT ATTENTION	① ② ③ ④ ⑤ ⑥ ⑦ ⑧ ⑨ ⑩
FORGETFUL / CONFUSIONED	① ② ③ ④ ⑤ ⑥ ⑦ ⑧ ⑨ ⑩

HYPERACTIVITY

CONSTANTLY MOVING / TALKING	① ② ③ ④ ⑤ ⑥ ⑦ ⑧ ⑨ ⑩
STRUGGLING TO SIT STILL	① ② ③ ④ ⑤ ⑥ ⑦ ⑧ ⑨ ⑩
TOUCHING THINGS REPEATEDLY	① ② ③ ④ ⑤ ⑥ ⑦ ⑧ ⑨ ⑩
DIFFICULT SLEEPING	① ② ③ ④ ⑤ ⑥ ⑦ ⑧ ⑨ ⑩

IMPULSIVITY

ACTING WITHOUT THINKING	① ② ③ ④ ⑤ ⑥ ⑦ ⑧ ⑨ ⑩
INTERRUPTING OTHERS	① ② ③ ④ ⑤ ⑥ ⑦ ⑧ ⑨ ⑩
EASILY FRUSTRATED	① ② ③ ④ ⑤ ⑥ ⑦ ⑧ ⑨ ⑩
UNABLE TO HOLD BACK EMOTIONS	① ② ③ ④ ⑤ ⑥ ⑦ ⑧ ⑨ ⑩

MEALS

MEDICATIONS

Water Tracker 🍼 🍼 🍼 🍼 🍼 🍼 🍼

NOTES

....
....

DAY GOALS

1 ....
2 ....
3 ....

DATE
WEEK
LOCATION
WEIGHT

Mood Tracker 😟 😐 😖 😢 😠 😃

BEHAVIOR

INATTENTION

SHORT ATTENTION	① ② ③ ④ ⑤ ⑥ ⑦ ⑧ ⑨ ⑩
UNMOTIVATED / BORED	① ② ③ ④ ⑤ ⑥ ⑦ ⑧ ⑨ ⑩
SHORT ATTENTION	① ② ③ ④ ⑤ ⑥ ⑦ ⑧ ⑨ ⑩
FORGETFUL / CONFUSIONED	① ② ③ ④ ⑤ ⑥ ⑦ ⑧ ⑨ ⑩

HYPERACTIVITY

CONSTANTLY MOVING / TALKING	① ② ③ ④ ⑤ ⑥ ⑦ ⑧ ⑨ ⑩
STRUGGLING TO SIT STILL	① ② ③ ④ ⑤ ⑥ ⑦ ⑧ ⑨ ⑩
TOUCHING THINGS REPEATEDLY	① ② ③ ④ ⑤ ⑥ ⑦ ⑧ ⑨ ⑩
DIFFICULT SLEEPING	① ② ③ ④ ⑤ ⑥ ⑦ ⑧ ⑨ ⑩

IMPULSIVITY

ACTING WITHOUT THINKING	① ② ③ ④ ⑤ ⑥ ⑦ ⑧ ⑨ ⑩
INTERRUPTING OTHERS	① ② ③ ④ ⑤ ⑥ ⑦ ⑧ ⑨ ⑩
EASILY FRUSTRATED	① ② ③ ④ ⑤ ⑥ ⑦ ⑧ ⑨ ⑩
UNABLE TO HOLD BACK EMOTIONS	① ② ③ ④ ⑤ ⑥ ⑦ ⑧ ⑨ ⑩

MEALS

MEDICATIONS

Water Tracker 🍼 🍼 🍼 🍼 🍼 🍼 🍼

NOTES

....
....

DAY GOALS

1 ....
2 ....
3 ....

DATE
WEEK
LOCATION
WEIGHT

Mood Tracker 😕 😐 😖 😢 😠 😃

BEHAVIOR

INATTENTION

SHORT ATTENTION	① ② ③ ④ ⑤ ⑥ ⑦ ⑧ ⑨ ⑩
UNMOTIVATED / BORED	① ② ③ ④ ⑤ ⑥ ⑦ ⑧ ⑨ ⑩
SHORT ATTENTION	① ② ③ ④ ⑤ ⑥ ⑦ ⑧ ⑨ ⑩
FORGETFUL / CONFUSIONED	① ② ③ ④ ⑤ ⑥ ⑦ ⑧ ⑨ ⑩

HYPERACTIVITY

CONSTANTLY MOVING / TALKING	① ② ③ ④ ⑤ ⑥ ⑦ ⑧ ⑨ ⑩
STRUGGLING TO SIT STILL	① ② ③ ④ ⑤ ⑥ ⑦ ⑧ ⑨ ⑩
TOUCHING THINGS REPEATEDLY	① ② ③ ④ ⑤ ⑥ ⑦ ⑧ ⑨ ⑩
DIFFICULT SLEEPING	① ② ③ ④ ⑤ ⑥ ⑦ ⑧ ⑨ ⑩

IMPULSIVITY

ACTING WITHOUT THINKING	① ② ③ ④ ⑤ ⑥ ⑦ ⑧ ⑨ ⑩
INTERRUPTING OTHERS	① ② ③ ④ ⑤ ⑥ ⑦ ⑧ ⑨ ⑩
EASILY FRUSTRATED	① ② ③ ④ ⑤ ⑥ ⑦ ⑧ ⑨ ⑩
UNABLE TO HOLD BACK EMOTIONS	① ② ③ ④ ⑤ ⑥ ⑦ ⑧ ⑨ ⑩

MEALS

MEDICATIONS

Water Tracker 🍼 🍼 🍼 🍼 🍼 🍼 🍼

NOTES

....
....

DAY GOALS

1 ....
2 ....
3 ....

DATE
WEEK
LOCATION
WEIGHT

Mood Tracker 😟 😐 😖 😢 😠 😃

BEHAVIOR

INATTENTION

SHORT ATTENTION	① ② ③ ④ ⑤ ⑥ ⑦ ⑧ ⑨ ⑩
UNMOTIVATED / BORED	① ② ③ ④ ⑤ ⑥ ⑦ ⑧ ⑨ ⑩
SHORT ATTENTION	① ② ③ ④ ⑤ ⑥ ⑦ ⑧ ⑨ ⑩
FORGETFUL / CONFUSIONED	① ② ③ ④ ⑤ ⑥ ⑦ ⑧ ⑨ ⑩

HYPERACTIVITY

CONSTANTLY MOVING / TALKING	① ② ③ ④ ⑤ ⑥ ⑦ ⑧ ⑨ ⑩
STRUGGLING TO SIT STILL	① ② ③ ④ ⑤ ⑥ ⑦ ⑧ ⑨ ⑩
TOUCHING THINGS REPEATEDLY	① ② ③ ④ ⑤ ⑥ ⑦ ⑧ ⑨ ⑩
DIFFICULT SLEEPING	① ② ③ ④ ⑤ ⑥ ⑦ ⑧ ⑨ ⑩

IMPULSIVITY

ACTING WITHOUT THINKING	① ② ③ ④ ⑤ ⑥ ⑦ ⑧ ⑨ ⑩
INTERRUPTING OTHERS	① ② ③ ④ ⑤ ⑥ ⑦ ⑧ ⑨ ⑩
EASILY FRUSTRATED	① ② ③ ④ ⑤ ⑥ ⑦ ⑧ ⑨ ⑩
UNABLE TO HOLD BACK EMOTIONS	① ② ③ ④ ⑤ ⑥ ⑦ ⑧ ⑨ ⑩

MEALS

MEDICATIONS

Water Tracker 🍼 🍼 🍼 🍼 🍼 🍼 🍼

NOTES

....
....

DAY GOALS

1 ....
2 ....
3 ....

DATE
WEEK
LOCATION
WEIGHT

Mood Tracker ☹ 😐 😖 😢 😠 😃

BEHAVIOR

INATTENTION

SHORT ATTENTION	① ② ③ ④ ⑤ ⑥ ⑦ ⑧ ⑨ ⑩
UNMOTIVATED / BORED	① ② ③ ④ ⑤ ⑥ ⑦ ⑧ ⑨ ⑩
SHORT ATTENTION	① ② ③ ④ ⑤ ⑥ ⑦ ⑧ ⑨ ⑩
FORGETFUL / CONFUSIONED	① ② ③ ④ ⑤ ⑥ ⑦ ⑧ ⑨ ⑩

HYPERACTIVITY

CONSTANTLY MOVING / TALKING	① ② ③ ④ ⑤ ⑥ ⑦ ⑧ ⑨ ⑩
STRUGGLING TO SIT STILL	① ② ③ ④ ⑤ ⑥ ⑦ ⑧ ⑨ ⑩
TOUCHING THINGS REPEATEDLY	① ② ③ ④ ⑤ ⑥ ⑦ ⑧ ⑨ ⑩
DIFFICULT SLEEPING	① ② ③ ④ ⑤ ⑥ ⑦ ⑧ ⑨ ⑩

IMPULSIVITY

ACTING WITHOUT THINKING	① ② ③ ④ ⑤ ⑥ ⑦ ⑧ ⑨ ⑩
INTERRUPTING OTHERS	① ② ③ ④ ⑤ ⑥ ⑦ ⑧ ⑨ ⑩
EASILY FRUSTRATED	① ② ③ ④ ⑤ ⑥ ⑦ ⑧ ⑨ ⑩
UNABLE TO HOLD BACK EMOTIONS	① ② ③ ④ ⑤ ⑥ ⑦ ⑧ ⑨ ⑩

MEALS	MEDICATIONS

Water Tracker 🍼 🍼 🍼 🍼 🍼 🍼 🍼

NOTES

....
....

DAY GOALS

1 ....
2 ....
3 ....

DATE
WEEK
LOCATION
WEIGHT

Mood Tracker

BEHAVIOR

INATTENTION

SHORT ATTENTION	① ② ③ ④ ⑤ ⑥ ⑦ ⑧ ⑨ ⑩
UNMOTIVATED / BORED	① ② ③ ④ ⑤ ⑥ ⑦ ⑧ ⑨ ⑩
SHORT ATTENTION	① ② ③ ④ ⑤ ⑥ ⑦ ⑧ ⑨ ⑩
FORGETFUL / CONFUSIONED	① ② ③ ④ ⑤ ⑥ ⑦ ⑧ ⑨ ⑩

HYPERACTIVITY

CONSTANTLY MOVING / TALKING	① ② ③ ④ ⑤ ⑥ ⑦ ⑧ ⑨ ⑩
STRUGGLING TO SIT STILL	① ② ③ ④ ⑤ ⑥ ⑦ ⑧ ⑨ ⑩
TOUCHING THINGS REPEATEDLY	① ② ③ ④ ⑤ ⑥ ⑦ ⑧ ⑨ ⑩
DIFFICULT SLEEPING	① ② ③ ④ ⑤ ⑥ ⑦ ⑧ ⑨ ⑩

IMPULSIVITY

ACTING WITHOUT THINKING	① ② ③ ④ ⑤ ⑥ ⑦ ⑧ ⑨ ⑩
INTERRUPTING OTHERS	① ② ③ ④ ⑤ ⑥ ⑦ ⑧ ⑨ ⑩
EASILY FRUSTRATED	① ② ③ ④ ⑤ ⑥ ⑦ ⑧ ⑨ ⑩
UNABLE TO HOLD BACK EMOTIONS	① ② ③ ④ ⑤ ⑥ ⑦ ⑧ ⑨ ⑩

MEALS

MEDICATIONS

Water Tracker

NOTES

....
....

DAY GOALS

1 ....
2 ....
3 ....

DATE
WEEK
LOCATION
WEIGHT

Mood Tracker ☹ 😐 😖 🥲 😠 😃

BEHAVIOR

INATTENTION

SHORT ATTENTION	① ② ③ ④ ⑤ ⑥ ⑦ ⑧ ⑨ ⑩
UNMOTIVATED / BORED	① ② ③ ④ ⑤ ⑥ ⑦ ⑧ ⑨ ⑩
SHORT ATTENTION	① ② ③ ④ ⑤ ⑥ ⑦ ⑧ ⑨ ⑩
FORGETFUL / CONFUSIONED	① ② ③ ④ ⑤ ⑥ ⑦ ⑧ ⑨ ⑩

HYPERACTIVITY

CONSTANTLY MOVING / TALKING	① ② ③ ④ ⑤ ⑥ ⑦ ⑧ ⑨ ⑩
STRUGGLING TO SIT STILL	① ② ③ ④ ⑤ ⑥ ⑦ ⑧ ⑨ ⑩
TOUCHING THINGS REPEATEDLY	① ② ③ ④ ⑤ ⑥ ⑦ ⑧ ⑨ ⑩
DIFFICULT SLEEPING	① ② ③ ④ ⑤ ⑥ ⑦ ⑧ ⑨ ⑩

IMPULSIVITY

ACTING WITHOUT THINKING	① ② ③ ④ ⑤ ⑥ ⑦ ⑧ ⑨ ⑩
INTERRUPTING OTHERS	① ② ③ ④ ⑤ ⑥ ⑦ ⑧ ⑨ ⑩
EASILY FRUSTRATED	① ② ③ ④ ⑤ ⑥ ⑦ ⑧ ⑨ ⑩
UNABLE TO HOLD BACK EMOTIONS	① ② ③ ④ ⑤ ⑥ ⑦ ⑧ ⑨ ⑩

MEALS

MEDICATIONS

Water Tracker 🍼 🍼 🍼 🍼 🍼 🍼 🍼

NOTES

....
....

DAY GOALS

1 ....
2 ....
3 ....

DATE
WEEK
LOCATION
WEIGHT

Mood Tracker 😞 😐 😖 😢 😠 😃

BEHAVIOR

INATTENTION

SHORT ATTENTION	① ② ③ ④ ⑤ ⑥ ⑦ ⑧ ⑨ ⑩
UNMOTIVATED / BORED	① ② ③ ④ ⑤ ⑥ ⑦ ⑧ ⑨ ⑩
SHORT ATTENTION	① ② ③ ④ ⑤ ⑥ ⑦ ⑧ ⑨ ⑩
FORGETFUL / CONFUSIONED	① ② ③ ④ ⑤ ⑥ ⑦ ⑧ ⑨ ⑩

HYPERACTIVITY

CONSTANTLY MOVING / TALKING	① ② ③ ④ ⑤ ⑥ ⑦ ⑧ ⑨ ⑩
STRUGGLING TO SIT STILL	① ② ③ ④ ⑤ ⑥ ⑦ ⑧ ⑨ ⑩
TOUCHING THINGS REPEATEDLY	① ② ③ ④ ⑤ ⑥ ⑦ ⑧ ⑨ ⑩
DIFFICULT SLEEPING	① ② ③ ④ ⑤ ⑥ ⑦ ⑧ ⑨ ⑩

IMPULSIVITY

ACTING WITHOUT THINKING	① ② ③ ④ ⑤ ⑥ ⑦ ⑧ ⑨ ⑩
INTERRUPTING OTHERS	① ② ③ ④ ⑤ ⑥ ⑦ ⑧ ⑨ ⑩
EASILY FRUSTRATED	① ② ③ ④ ⑤ ⑥ ⑦ ⑧ ⑨ ⑩
UNABLE TO HOLD BACK EMOTIONS	① ② ③ ④ ⑤ ⑥ ⑦ ⑧ ⑨ ⑩

MEALS

MEDICATIONS

Water Tracker 🧴 🧴 🧴 🧴 🧴 🧴 🧴

NOTES

....
....

DAY GOALS	
1	....
2	....
3	....

DATE
WEEK
LOCATION
WEIGHT

Mood Tracker

BEHAVIOR

INATTENTION

SHORT ATTENTION	① ② ③ ④ ⑤ ⑥ ⑦ ⑧ ⑨ ⑩
UNMOTIVATED / BORED	① ② ③ ④ ⑤ ⑥ ⑦ ⑧ ⑨ ⑩
SHORT ATTENTION	① ② ③ ④ ⑤ ⑥ ⑦ ⑧ ⑨ ⑩
FORGETFUL / CONFUSIONED	① ② ③ ④ ⑤ ⑥ ⑦ ⑧ ⑨ ⑩

HYPERACTIVITY

CONSTANTLY MOVING / TALKING	① ② ③ ④ ⑤ ⑥ ⑦ ⑧ ⑨ ⑩
STRUGGLING TO SIT STILL	① ② ③ ④ ⑤ ⑥ ⑦ ⑧ ⑨ ⑩
TOUCHING THINGS REPEATEDLY	① ② ③ ④ ⑤ ⑥ ⑦ ⑧ ⑨ ⑩
DIFFICULT SLEEPING	① ② ③ ④ ⑤ ⑥ ⑦ ⑧ ⑨ ⑩

IMPULSIVITY

ACTING WITHOUT THINKING	① ② ③ ④ ⑤ ⑥ ⑦ ⑧ ⑨ ⑩
INTERRUPTING OTHERS	① ② ③ ④ ⑤ ⑥ ⑦ ⑧ ⑨ ⑩
EASILY FRUSTRATED	① ② ③ ④ ⑤ ⑥ ⑦ ⑧ ⑨ ⑩
UNABLE TO HOLD BACK EMOTIONS	① ② ③ ④ ⑤ ⑥ ⑦ ⑧ ⑨ ⑩

MEALS	MEDICATIONS

Water Tracker

NOTES

....
....

DAY GOALS	
1	
2	
3	

DATE
WEEK
LOCATION
WEIGHT

Mood Tracker   😟 😐 😖 😢 😠 😃

BEHAVIOR

INATTENTION

SHORT ATTENTION	① ② ③ ④ ⑤ ⑥ ⑦ ⑧ ⑨ ⑩
UNMOTIVATED / BORED	① ② ③ ④ ⑤ ⑥ ⑦ ⑧ ⑨ ⑩
SHORT ATTENTION	① ② ③ ④ ⑤ ⑥ ⑦ ⑧ ⑨ ⑩
FORGETFUL / CONFUSIONED	① ② ③ ④ ⑤ ⑥ ⑦ ⑧ ⑨ ⑩

HYPERACTIVITY

CONSTANTLY MOVING / TALKING	① ② ③ ④ ⑤ ⑥ ⑦ ⑧ ⑨ ⑩
STRUGGLING TO SIT STILL	① ② ③ ④ ⑤ ⑥ ⑦ ⑧ ⑨ ⑩
TOUCHING THINGS REPEATEDLY	① ② ③ ④ ⑤ ⑥ ⑦ ⑧ ⑨ ⑩
DIFFICULT SLEEPING	① ② ③ ④ ⑤ ⑥ ⑦ ⑧ ⑨ ⑩

IMPULSIVITY

ACTING WITHOUT THINKING	① ② ③ ④ ⑤ ⑥ ⑦ ⑧ ⑨ ⑩
INTERRUPTING OTHERS	① ② ③ ④ ⑤ ⑥ ⑦ ⑧ ⑨ ⑩
EASILY FRUSTRATED	① ② ③ ④ ⑤ ⑥ ⑦ ⑧ ⑨ ⑩
UNABLE TO HOLD BACK EMOTIONS	① ② ③ ④ ⑤ ⑥ ⑦ ⑧ ⑨ ⑩

MEALS	MEDICATIONS

Water Tracker 🍼 🍼 🍼 🍼 🍼 🍼 🍼

NOTES

....
....

DAY GOALS	
1	DATE
2	WEEK
3	LOCATION
	WEIGHT

Mood Tracker 😟 😐 😖 😢 😠 😃

BEHAVIOR

INATTENTION

SHORT ATTENTION	① ② ③ ④ ⑤ ⑥ ⑦ ⑧ ⑨ ⑩
UNMOTIVATED / BORED	① ② ③ ④ ⑤ ⑥ ⑦ ⑧ ⑨ ⑩
SHORT ATTENTION	① ② ③ ④ ⑤ ⑥ ⑦ ⑧ ⑨ ⑩
FORGETFUL / CONFUSIONED	① ② ③ ④ ⑤ ⑥ ⑦ ⑧ ⑨ ⑩

HYPERACTIVITY

CONSTANTLY MOVING / TALKING	① ② ③ ④ ⑤ ⑥ ⑦ ⑧ ⑨ ⑩
STRUGGLING TO SIT STILL	① ② ③ ④ ⑤ ⑥ ⑦ ⑧ ⑨ ⑩
TOUCHING THINGS REPEATEDLY	① ② ③ ④ ⑤ ⑥ ⑦ ⑧ ⑨ ⑩
DIFFICULT SLEEPING	① ② ③ ④ ⑤ ⑥ ⑦ ⑧ ⑨ ⑩

IMPULSIVITY

ACTING WITHOUT THINKING	① ② ③ ④ ⑤ ⑥ ⑦ ⑧ ⑨ ⑩
INTERRUPTING OTHERS	① ② ③ ④ ⑤ ⑥ ⑦ ⑧ ⑨ ⑩
EASILY FRUSTRATED	① ② ③ ④ ⑤ ⑥ ⑦ ⑧ ⑨ ⑩
UNABLE TO HOLD BACK EMOTIONS	① ② ③ ④ ⑤ ⑥ ⑦ ⑧ ⑨ ⑩

MEALS	MEDICATIONS

Water Tracker 🍼 🍼 🍼 🍼 🍼 🍼 🍼

NOTES

....
....

DAY GOALS

1 ....
2 ....
3 ....

DATE
WEEK
LOCATION
WEIGHT

Mood Tracker 😟 😐 😖 😢 😠 😃

BEHAVIOR

INATTENTION

SHORT ATTENTION	① ② ③ ④ ⑤ ⑥ ⑦ ⑧ ⑨ ⑩
UNMOTIVATED / BORED	① ② ③ ④ ⑤ ⑥ ⑦ ⑧ ⑨ ⑩
SHORT ATTENTION	① ② ③ ④ ⑤ ⑥ ⑦ ⑧ ⑨ ⑩
FORGETFUL / CONFUSIONED	① ② ③ ④ ⑤ ⑥ ⑦ ⑧ ⑨ ⑩

HYPERACTIVITY

CONSTANTLY MOVING / TALKING	① ② ③ ④ ⑤ ⑥ ⑦ ⑧ ⑨ ⑩
STRUGGLING TO SIT STILL	① ② ③ ④ ⑤ ⑥ ⑦ ⑧ ⑨ ⑩
TOUCHING THINGS REPEATEDLY	① ② ③ ④ ⑤ ⑥ ⑦ ⑧ ⑨ ⑩
DIFFICULT SLEEPING	① ② ③ ④ ⑤ ⑥ ⑦ ⑧ ⑨ ⑩

IMPULSIVITY

ACTING WITHOUT THINKING	① ② ③ ④ ⑤ ⑥ ⑦ ⑧ ⑨ ⑩
INTERRUPTING OTHERS	① ② ③ ④ ⑤ ⑥ ⑦ ⑧ ⑨ ⑩
EASILY FRUSTRATED	① ② ③ ④ ⑤ ⑥ ⑦ ⑧ ⑨ ⑩
UNABLE TO HOLD BACK EMOTIONS	① ② ③ ④ ⑤ ⑥ ⑦ ⑧ ⑨ ⑩

MEALS

MEDICATIONS

Water Tracker 🍼 🍼 🍼 🍼 🍼 🍼 🍼

NOTES

....
....

DAY GOALS	
1	DATE
2	WEEK
3	LOCATION
	WEIGHT

Mood Tracker 😕 😐 😖 😢 😠 😀

BEHAVIOR

INATTENTION

SHORT ATTENTION	① ② ③ ④ ⑤ ⑥ ⑦ ⑧ ⑨ ⑩
UNMOTIVATED / BORED	① ② ③ ④ ⑤ ⑥ ⑦ ⑧ ⑨ ⑩
SHORT ATTENTION	① ② ③ ④ ⑤ ⑥ ⑦ ⑧ ⑨ ⑩
FORGETFUL / CONFUSIONED	① ② ③ ④ ⑤ ⑥ ⑦ ⑧ ⑨ ⑩

HYPERACTIVITY

CONSTANTLY MOVING / TALKING	① ② ③ ④ ⑤ ⑥ ⑦ ⑧ ⑨ ⑩
STRUGGLING TO SIT STILL	① ② ③ ④ ⑤ ⑥ ⑦ ⑧ ⑨ ⑩
TOUCHING THINGS REPEATEDLY	① ② ③ ④ ⑤ ⑥ ⑦ ⑧ ⑨ ⑩
DIFFICULT SLEEPING	① ② ③ ④ ⑤ ⑥ ⑦ ⑧ ⑨ ⑩

IMPULSIVITY

ACTING WITHOUT THINKING	① ② ③ ④ ⑤ ⑥ ⑦ ⑧ ⑨ ⑩
INTERRUPTING OTHERS	① ② ③ ④ ⑤ ⑥ ⑦ ⑧ ⑨ ⑩
EASILY FRUSTRATED	① ② ③ ④ ⑤ ⑥ ⑦ ⑧ ⑨ ⑩
UNABLE TO HOLD BACK EMOTIONS	① ② ③ ④ ⑤ ⑥ ⑦ ⑧ ⑨ ⑩

MEALS	MEDICATIONS

Water Tracker 🍼 🍼 🍼 🍼 🍼 🍼 🍼

NOTES

....
....

DAY GOALS	
1	
2	
3	

DATE
WEEK
LOCATION
WEIGHT

Mood Tracker 😟 😐 😖 😢 😠 😃

BEHAVIOR

INATTENTION

SHORT ATTENTION	① ② ③ ④ ⑤ ⑥ ⑦ ⑧ ⑨ ⑩
UNMOTIVATED / BORED	① ② ③ ④ ⑤ ⑥ ⑦ ⑧ ⑨ ⑩
SHORT ATTENTION	① ② ③ ④ ⑤ ⑥ ⑦ ⑧ ⑨ ⑩
FORGETFUL / CONFUSIONED	① ② ③ ④ ⑤ ⑥ ⑦ ⑧ ⑨ ⑩

HYPERACTIVITY

CONSTANTLY MOVING / TALKING	① ② ③ ④ ⑤ ⑥ ⑦ ⑧ ⑨ ⑩
STRUGGLING TO SIT STILL	① ② ③ ④ ⑤ ⑥ ⑦ ⑧ ⑨ ⑩
TOUCHING THINGS REPEATEDLY	① ② ③ ④ ⑤ ⑥ ⑦ ⑧ ⑨ ⑩
DIFFICULT SLEEPING	① ② ③ ④ ⑤ ⑥ ⑦ ⑧ ⑨ ⑩

IMPULSIVITY

ACTING WITHOUT THINKING	① ② ③ ④ ⑤ ⑥ ⑦ ⑧ ⑨ ⑩
INTERRUPTING OTHERS	① ② ③ ④ ⑤ ⑥ ⑦ ⑧ ⑨ ⑩
EASILY FRUSTRATED	① ② ③ ④ ⑤ ⑥ ⑦ ⑧ ⑨ ⑩
UNABLE TO HOLD BACK EMOTIONS	① ② ③ ④ ⑤ ⑥ ⑦ ⑧ ⑨ ⑩

MEALS	MEDICATIONS

Water Tracker 🍼 🍼 🍼 🍼 🍼 🍼 🍼

NOTES
....
....

DAY GOALS	
1	
2	
3	

DATE
WEEK
LOCATION
WEIGHT

Mood Tracker ☹ 😐 😖 😢 😠 😃

BEHAVIOR

INATTENTION

SHORT ATTENTION	① ② ③ ④ ⑤ ⑥ ⑦ ⑧ ⑨ ⑩
UNMOTIVATED / BORED	① ② ③ ④ ⑤ ⑥ ⑦ ⑧ ⑨ ⑩
SHORT ATTENTION	① ② ③ ④ ⑤ ⑥ ⑦ ⑧ ⑨ ⑩
FORGETFUL / CONFUSIONED	① ② ③ ④ ⑤ ⑥ ⑦ ⑧ ⑨ ⑩

HYPERACTIVITY

CONSTANTLY MOVING / TALKING	① ② ③ ④ ⑤ ⑥ ⑦ ⑧ ⑨ ⑩
STRUGGLING TO SIT STILL	① ② ③ ④ ⑤ ⑥ ⑦ ⑧ ⑨ ⑩
TOUCHING THINGS REPEATEDLY	① ② ③ ④ ⑤ ⑥ ⑦ ⑧ ⑨ ⑩
DIFFICULT SLEEPING	① ② ③ ④ ⑤ ⑥ ⑦ ⑧ ⑨ ⑩

IMPULSIVITY

ACTING WITHOUT THINKING	① ② ③ ④ ⑤ ⑥ ⑦ ⑧ ⑨ ⑩
INTERRUPTING OTHERS	① ② ③ ④ ⑤ ⑥ ⑦ ⑧ ⑨ ⑩
EASILY FRUSTRATED	① ② ③ ④ ⑤ ⑥ ⑦ ⑧ ⑨ ⑩
UNABLE TO HOLD BACK EMOTIONS	① ② ③ ④ ⑤ ⑥ ⑦ ⑧ ⑨ ⑩

MEALS	MEDICATIONS

Water Tracker 🍼 🍼 🍼 🍼 🍼 🍼 🍼

NOTES

....
....

DAY GOALS	
1	DATE
2	WEEK
3	LOCATION
	WEIGHT

Mood Tracker 😕 😐 😖 😢 😠 😃

BEHAVIOR

INATTENTION

SHORT ATTENTION	① ② ③ ④ ⑤ ⑥ ⑦ ⑧ ⑨ ⑩
UNMOTIVATED / BORED	① ② ③ ④ ⑤ ⑥ ⑦ ⑧ ⑨ ⑩
SHORT ATTENTION	① ② ③ ④ ⑤ ⑥ ⑦ ⑧ ⑨ ⑩
FORGETFUL / CONFUSIONED	① ② ③ ④ ⑤ ⑥ ⑦ ⑧ ⑨ ⑩

HYPERACTIVITY

CONSTANTLY MOVING / TALKING	① ② ③ ④ ⑤ ⑥ ⑦ ⑧ ⑨ ⑩
STRUGGLING TO SIT STILL	① ② ③ ④ ⑤ ⑥ ⑦ ⑧ ⑨ ⑩
TOUCHING THINGS REPEATEDLY	① ② ③ ④ ⑤ ⑥ ⑦ ⑧ ⑨ ⑩
DIFFICULT SLEEPING	① ② ③ ④ ⑤ ⑥ ⑦ ⑧ ⑨ ⑩

IMPULSIVITY

ACTING WITHOUT THINKING	① ② ③ ④ ⑤ ⑥ ⑦ ⑧ ⑨ ⑩
INTERRUPTING OTHERS	① ② ③ ④ ⑤ ⑥ ⑦ ⑧ ⑨ ⑩
EASILY FRUSTRATED	① ② ③ ④ ⑤ ⑥ ⑦ ⑧ ⑨ ⑩
UNABLE TO HOLD BACK EMOTIONS	① ② ③ ④ ⑤ ⑥ ⑦ ⑧ ⑨ ⑩

MEALS	MEDICATIONS

Water Tracker 🍼 🍼 🍼 🍼 🍼 🍼 🍼

NOTES

....
....

DAY GOALS	DATE
1	WEEK
2	LOCATION
3	WEIGHT

Mood Tracker ☹ 😐 😣 😢 😠 😃

BEHAVIOR

INATTENTION

SHORT ATTENTION	① ② ③ ④ ⑤ ⑥ ⑦ ⑧ ⑨ ⑩
UNMOTIVATED / BORED	① ② ③ ④ ⑤ ⑥ ⑦ ⑧ ⑨ ⑩
SHORT ATTENTION	① ② ③ ④ ⑤ ⑥ ⑦ ⑧ ⑨ ⑩
FORGETFUL / CONFUSIONED	① ② ③ ④ ⑤ ⑥ ⑦ ⑧ ⑨ ⑩

HYPERACTIVITY

CONSTANTLY MOVING / TALKING	① ② ③ ④ ⑤ ⑥ ⑦ ⑧ ⑨ ⑩
STRUGGLING TO SIT STILL	① ② ③ ④ ⑤ ⑥ ⑦ ⑧ ⑨ ⑩
TOUCHING THINGS REPEATEDLY	① ② ③ ④ ⑤ ⑥ ⑦ ⑧ ⑨ ⑩
DIFFICULT SLEEPING	① ② ③ ④ ⑤ ⑥ ⑦ ⑧ ⑨ ⑩

IMPULSIVITY

ACTING WITHOUT THINKING	① ② ③ ④ ⑤ ⑥ ⑦ ⑧ ⑨ ⑩
INTERRUPTING OTHERS	① ② ③ ④ ⑤ ⑥ ⑦ ⑧ ⑨ ⑩
EASILY FRUSTRATED	① ② ③ ④ ⑤ ⑥ ⑦ ⑧ ⑨ ⑩
UNABLE TO HOLD BACK EMOTIONS	① ② ③ ④ ⑤ ⑥ ⑦ ⑧ ⑨ ⑩

MEALS	MEDICATIONS

Water Tracker 🍼 🍼 🍼 🍼 🍼 🍼 🍼

NOTES

....
....

DAY GOALS

1 ....
2 ....
3 ....

DATE
WEEK
LOCATION
WEIGHT

Mood Tracker ☹️ 😐 😖 😢 😠 😃

BEHAVIOR

INATTENTION

SHORT ATTENTION	① ② ③ ④ ⑤ ⑥ ⑦ ⑧ ⑨ ⑩
UNMOTIVATED / BORED	① ② ③ ④ ⑤ ⑥ ⑦ ⑧ ⑨ ⑩
SHORT ATTENTION	① ② ③ ④ ⑤ ⑥ ⑦ ⑧ ⑨ ⑩
FORGETFUL / CONFUSIONED	① ② ③ ④ ⑤ ⑥ ⑦ ⑧ ⑨ ⑩

HYPERACTIVITY

CONSTANTLY MOVING / TALKING	① ② ③ ④ ⑤ ⑥ ⑦ ⑧ ⑨ ⑩
STRUGGLING TO SIT STILL	① ② ③ ④ ⑤ ⑥ ⑦ ⑧ ⑨ ⑩
TOUCHING THINGS REPEATEDLY	① ② ③ ④ ⑤ ⑥ ⑦ ⑧ ⑨ ⑩
DIFFICULT SLEEPING	① ② ③ ④ ⑤ ⑥ ⑦ ⑧ ⑨ ⑩

IMPULSIVITY

ACTING WITHOUT THINKING	① ② ③ ④ ⑤ ⑥ ⑦ ⑧ ⑨ ⑩
INTERRUPTING OTHERS	① ② ③ ④ ⑤ ⑥ ⑦ ⑧ ⑨ ⑩
EASILY FRUSTRATED	① ② ③ ④ ⑤ ⑥ ⑦ ⑧ ⑨ ⑩
UNABLE TO HOLD BACK EMOTIONS	① ② ③ ④ ⑤ ⑥ ⑦ ⑧ ⑨ ⑩

MEALS	MEDICATIONS

Water Tracker 🍼 🍼 🍼 🍼 🍼 🍼 🍼

NOTES

....
....

DAY GOALS

1 ....
2 ....
3 ....

DATE
WEEK
LOCATION
WEIGHT

Mood Tracker ☹️ 😐 😖 💧 😠 😃

BEHAVIOR

INATTENTION

SHORT ATTENTION	① ② ③ ④ ⑤ ⑥ ⑦ ⑧ ⑨ ⑩
UNMOTIVATED / BORED	① ② ③ ④ ⑤ ⑥ ⑦ ⑧ ⑨ ⑩
SHORT ATTENTION	① ② ③ ④ ⑤ ⑥ ⑦ ⑧ ⑨ ⑩
FORGETFUL / CONFUSIONED	① ② ③ ④ ⑤ ⑥ ⑦ ⑧ ⑨ ⑩

HYPERACTIVITY

CONSTANTLY MOVING / TALKING	① ② ③ ④ ⑤ ⑥ ⑦ ⑧ ⑨ ⑩
STRUGGLING TO SIT STILL	① ② ③ ④ ⑤ ⑥ ⑦ ⑧ ⑨ ⑩
TOUCHING THINGS REPEATEDLY	① ② ③ ④ ⑤ ⑥ ⑦ ⑧ ⑨ ⑩
DIFFICULT SLEEPING	① ② ③ ④ ⑤ ⑥ ⑦ ⑧ ⑨ ⑩

IMPULSIVITY

ACTING WITHOUT THINKING	① ② ③ ④ ⑤ ⑥ ⑦ ⑧ ⑨ ⑩
INTERRUPTING OTHERS	① ② ③ ④ ⑤ ⑥ ⑦ ⑧ ⑨ ⑩
EASILY FRUSTRATED	① ② ③ ④ ⑤ ⑥ ⑦ ⑧ ⑨ ⑩
UNABLE TO HOLD BACK EMOTIONS	① ② ③ ④ ⑤ ⑥ ⑦ ⑧ ⑨ ⑩

MEALS

MEDICATIONS

Water Tracker 🍼 🍼 🍼 🍼 🍼 🍼 🍼

NOTES

....
....

DAY GOALS	
1	DATE
2	WEEK
3	LOCATION
	WEIGHT

Mood Tracker ☹ 😐 😖 😢 😠 😃

BEHAVIOR

INATTENTION

SHORT ATTENTION	① ② ③ ④ ⑤ ⑥ ⑦ ⑧ ⑨ ⑩
UNMOTIVATED / BORED	① ② ③ ④ ⑤ ⑥ ⑦ ⑧ ⑨ ⑩
SHORT ATTENTION	① ② ③ ④ ⑤ ⑥ ⑦ ⑧ ⑨ ⑩
FORGETFUL / CONFUSIONED	① ② ③ ④ ⑤ ⑥ ⑦ ⑧ ⑨ ⑩

HYPERACTIVITY

CONSTANTLY MOVING / TALKING	① ② ③ ④ ⑤ ⑥ ⑦ ⑧ ⑨ ⑩
STRUGGLING TO SIT STILL	① ② ③ ④ ⑤ ⑥ ⑦ ⑧ ⑨ ⑩
TOUCHING THINGS REPEATEDLY	① ② ③ ④ ⑤ ⑥ ⑦ ⑧ ⑨ ⑩
DIFFICULT SLEEPING	① ② ③ ④ ⑤ ⑥ ⑦ ⑧ ⑨ ⑩

IMPULSIVITY

ACTING WITHOUT THINKING	① ② ③ ④ ⑤ ⑥ ⑦ ⑧ ⑨ ⑩
INTERRUPTING OTHERS	① ② ③ ④ ⑤ ⑥ ⑦ ⑧ ⑨ ⑩
EASILY FRUSTRATED	① ② ③ ④ ⑤ ⑥ ⑦ ⑧ ⑨ ⑩
UNABLE TO HOLD BACK EMOTIONS	① ② ③ ④ ⑤ ⑥ ⑦ ⑧ ⑨ ⑩

MEALS	MEDICATIONS

Water Tracker 🧴 🧴 🧴 🧴 🧴 🧴 🧴

NOTES

....
....

DAY GOALS	
1	
2	
3	

DATE
WEEK
LOCATION
WEIGHT

Mood Tracker 😕 😐 😣 😢 😠 😃

BEHAVIOR

INATTENTION

SHORT ATTENTION	① ② ③ ④ ⑤ ⑥ ⑦ ⑧ ⑨ ⑩
UNMOTIVATED / BORED	① ② ③ ④ ⑤ ⑥ ⑦ ⑧ ⑨ ⑩
SHORT ATTENTION	① ② ③ ④ ⑤ ⑥ ⑦ ⑧ ⑨ ⑩
FORGETFUL / CONFUSIONED	① ② ③ ④ ⑤ ⑥ ⑦ ⑧ ⑨ ⑩

HYPERACTIVITY

CONSTANTLY MOVING / TALKING	① ② ③ ④ ⑤ ⑥ ⑦ ⑧ ⑨ ⑩
STRUGGLING TO SIT STILL	① ② ③ ④ ⑤ ⑥ ⑦ ⑧ ⑨ ⑩
TOUCHING THINGS REPEATEDLY	① ② ③ ④ ⑤ ⑥ ⑦ ⑧ ⑨ ⑩
DIFFICULT SLEEPING	① ② ③ ④ ⑤ ⑥ ⑦ ⑧ ⑨ ⑩

IMPULSIVITY

ACTING WITHOUT THINKING	① ② ③ ④ ⑤ ⑥ ⑦ ⑧ ⑨ ⑩
INTERRUPTING OTHERS	① ② ③ ④ ⑤ ⑥ ⑦ ⑧ ⑨ ⑩
EASILY FRUSTRATED	① ② ③ ④ ⑤ ⑥ ⑦ ⑧ ⑨ ⑩
UNABLE TO HOLD BACK EMOTIONS	① ② ③ ④ ⑤ ⑥ ⑦ ⑧ ⑨ ⑩

MEALS	**MEDICATIONS**

Water Tracker 🍼 🍼 🍼 🍼 🍼 🍼 🍼

NOTES

....
....

DAY GOALS

1 ....
2 ....
3 ....

DATE
WEEK
LOCATION
WEIGHT

Mood Tracker

BEHAVIOR

INATTENTION

SHORT ATTENTION	① ② ③ ④ ⑤ ⑥ ⑦ ⑧ ⑨ ⑩
UNMOTIVATED / BORED	① ② ③ ④ ⑤ ⑥ ⑦ ⑧ ⑨ ⑩
SHORT ATTENTION	① ② ③ ④ ⑤ ⑥ ⑦ ⑧ ⑨ ⑩
FORGETFUL / CONFUSIONED	① ② ③ ④ ⑤ ⑥ ⑦ ⑧ ⑨ ⑩

HYPERACTIVITY

CONSTANTLY MOVING / TALKING	① ② ③ ④ ⑤ ⑥ ⑦ ⑧ ⑨ ⑩
STRUGGLING TO SIT STILL	① ② ③ ④ ⑤ ⑥ ⑦ ⑧ ⑨ ⑩
TOUCHING THINGS REPEATEDLY	① ② ③ ④ ⑤ ⑥ ⑦ ⑧ ⑨ ⑩
DIFFICULT SLEEPING	① ② ③ ④ ⑤ ⑥ ⑦ ⑧ ⑨ ⑩

IMPULSIVITY

ACTING WITHOUT THINKING	① ② ③ ④ ⑤ ⑥ ⑦ ⑧ ⑨ ⑩
INTERRUPTING OTHERS	① ② ③ ④ ⑤ ⑥ ⑦ ⑧ ⑨ ⑩
EASILY FRUSTRATED	① ② ③ ④ ⑤ ⑥ ⑦ ⑧ ⑨ ⑩
UNABLE TO HOLD BACK EMOTIONS	① ② ③ ④ ⑤ ⑥ ⑦ ⑧ ⑨ ⑩

MEALS

MEDICATIONS

Water Tracker

NOTES

....
....

DAY GOALS

1 ....
2 ....
3 ....

DATE
WEEK
LOCATION
WEIGHT

Mood Tracker 😕 😐 😖 😟 😠 😃

BEHAVIOR

INATTENTION

SHORT ATTENTION	① ② ③ ④ ⑤ ⑥ ⑦ ⑧ ⑨ ⑩
UNMOTIVATED / BORED	① ② ③ ④ ⑤ ⑥ ⑦ ⑧ ⑨ ⑩
SHORT ATTENTION	① ② ③ ④ ⑤ ⑥ ⑦ ⑧ ⑨ ⑩
FORGETFUL / CONFUSIONED	① ② ③ ④ ⑤ ⑥ ⑦ ⑧ ⑨ ⑩

HYPERACTIVITY

CONSTANTLY MOVING / TALKING	① ② ③ ④ ⑤ ⑥ ⑦ ⑧ ⑨ ⑩
STRUGGLING TO SIT STILL	① ② ③ ④ ⑤ ⑥ ⑦ ⑧ ⑨ ⑩
TOUCHING THINGS REPEATEDLY	① ② ③ ④ ⑤ ⑥ ⑦ ⑧ ⑨ ⑩
DIFFICULT SLEEPING	① ② ③ ④ ⑤ ⑥ ⑦ ⑧ ⑨ ⑩

IMPULSIVITY

ACTING WITHOUT THINKING	① ② ③ ④ ⑤ ⑥ ⑦ ⑧ ⑨ ⑩
INTERRUPTING OTHERS	① ② ③ ④ ⑤ ⑥ ⑦ ⑧ ⑨ ⑩
EASILY FRUSTRATED	① ② ③ ④ ⑤ ⑥ ⑦ ⑧ ⑨ ⑩
UNABLE TO HOLD BACK EMOTIONS	① ② ③ ④ ⑤ ⑥ ⑦ ⑧ ⑨ ⑩

MEALS

MEDICATIONS

Water Tracker 🍼 🍼 🍼 🍼 🍼 🍼 🍼

NOTES

....
....

DAY GOALS	
1	
2	
3	

DATE
WEEK
LOCATION
WEIGHT

Mood Tracker 😕 😐 😖 😢 😠 😃

BEHAVIOR

INATTENTION

SHORT ATTENTION	① ② ③ ④ ⑤ ⑥ ⑦ ⑧ ⑨ ⑩
UNMOTIVATED / BORED	① ② ③ ④ ⑤ ⑥ ⑦ ⑧ ⑨ ⑩
SHORT ATTENTION	① ② ③ ④ ⑤ ⑥ ⑦ ⑧ ⑨ ⑩
FORGETFUL / CONFUSIONED	① ② ③ ④ ⑤ ⑥ ⑦ ⑧ ⑨ ⑩

HYPERACTIVITY

CONSTANTLY MOVING / TALKING	① ② ③ ④ ⑤ ⑥ ⑦ ⑧ ⑨ ⑩
STRUGGLING TO SIT STILL	① ② ③ ④ ⑤ ⑥ ⑦ ⑧ ⑨ ⑩
TOUCHING THINGS REPEATEDLY	① ② ③ ④ ⑤ ⑥ ⑦ ⑧ ⑨ ⑩
DIFFICULT SLEEPING	① ② ③ ④ ⑤ ⑥ ⑦ ⑧ ⑨ ⑩

IMPULSIVITY

ACTING WITHOUT THINKING	① ② ③ ④ ⑤ ⑥ ⑦ ⑧ ⑨ ⑩
INTERRUPTING OTHERS	① ② ③ ④ ⑤ ⑥ ⑦ ⑧ ⑨ ⑩
EASILY FRUSTRATED	① ② ③ ④ ⑤ ⑥ ⑦ ⑧ ⑨ ⑩
UNABLE TO HOLD BACK EMOTIONS	① ② ③ ④ ⑤ ⑥ ⑦ ⑧ ⑨ ⑩

MEALS	MEDICATIONS

Water Tracker 🍼 🍼 🍼 🍼 🍼 🍼 🍼

NOTES

....
....

DAY GOALS	
1	
2	
3	

DATE ....
WEEK ....
LOCATION ....
WEIGHT ....

Mood Tracker 😕 😐 😣 😢 😠 😀

BEHAVIOR

INATTENTION

SHORT ATTENTION	① ② ③ ④ ⑤ ⑥ ⑦ ⑧ ⑨ ⑩
UNMOTIVATED / BORED	① ② ③ ④ ⑤ ⑥ ⑦ ⑧ ⑨ ⑩
SHORT ATTENTION	① ② ③ ④ ⑤ ⑥ ⑦ ⑧ ⑨ ⑩
FORGETFUL / CONFUSIONED	① ② ③ ④ ⑤ ⑥ ⑦ ⑧ ⑨ ⑩

HYPERACTIVITY

CONSTANTLY MOVING / TALKING	① ② ③ ④ ⑤ ⑥ ⑦ ⑧ ⑨ ⑩
STRUGGLING TO SIT STILL	① ② ③ ④ ⑤ ⑥ ⑦ ⑧ ⑨ ⑩
TOUCHING THINGS REPEATEDLY	① ② ③ ④ ⑤ ⑥ ⑦ ⑧ ⑨ ⑩
DIFFICULT SLEEPING	① ② ③ ④ ⑤ ⑥ ⑦ ⑧ ⑨ ⑩

IMPULSIVITY

ACTING WITHOUT THINKING	① ② ③ ④ ⑤ ⑥ ⑦ ⑧ ⑨ ⑩
INTERRUPTING OTHERS	① ② ③ ④ ⑤ ⑥ ⑦ ⑧ ⑨ ⑩
EASILY FRUSTRATED	① ② ③ ④ ⑤ ⑥ ⑦ ⑧ ⑨ ⑩
UNABLE TO HOLD BACK EMOTIONS	① ② ③ ④ ⑤ ⑥ ⑦ ⑧ ⑨ ⑩

MEALS	MEDICATIONS

Water Tracker 🍼 🍼 🍼 🍼 🍼 🍼 🍼

NOTES

....
....

DAY GOALS	
1	
2	
3	

DATE
WEEK
LOCATION
WEIGHT

Mood Tracker 😕 😐 😖 😢 😠 😃

BEHAVIOR

INATTENTION

SHORT ATTENTION	① ② ③ ④ ⑤ ⑥ ⑦ ⑧ ⑨ ⑩
UNMOTIVATED / BORED	① ② ③ ④ ⑤ ⑥ ⑦ ⑧ ⑨ ⑩
SHORT ATTENTION	① ② ③ ④ ⑤ ⑥ ⑦ ⑧ ⑨ ⑩
FORGETFUL / CONFUSIONED	① ② ③ ④ ⑤ ⑥ ⑦ ⑧ ⑨ ⑩

HYPERACTIVITY

CONSTANTLY MOVING / TALKING	① ② ③ ④ ⑤ ⑥ ⑦ ⑧ ⑨ ⑩
STRUGGLING TO SIT STILL	① ② ③ ④ ⑤ ⑥ ⑦ ⑧ ⑨ ⑩
TOUCHING THINGS REPEATEDLY	① ② ③ ④ ⑤ ⑥ ⑦ ⑧ ⑨ ⑩
DIFFICULT SLEEPING	① ② ③ ④ ⑤ ⑥ ⑦ ⑧ ⑨ ⑩

IMPULSIVITY

ACTING WITHOUT THINKING	① ② ③ ④ ⑤ ⑥ ⑦ ⑧ ⑨ ⑩
INTERRUPTING OTHERS	① ② ③ ④ ⑤ ⑥ ⑦ ⑧ ⑨ ⑩
EASILY FRUSTRATED	① ② ③ ④ ⑤ ⑥ ⑦ ⑧ ⑨ ⑩
UNABLE TO HOLD BACK EMOTIONS	① ② ③ ④ ⑤ ⑥ ⑦ ⑧ ⑨ ⑩

MEALS	MEDICATIONS

Water Tracker 🍼 🍼 🍼 🍼 🍼 🍼 🍼

NOTES

....
....

DAY GOALS	
1	
2	
3	

DATE ....
WEEK ....
LOCATION ....
WEIGHT ....

Mood Tracker 😟 😐 😖 😢 😠 😃

BEHAVIOR

INATTENTION

SHORT ATTENTION	① ② ③ ④ ⑤ ⑥ ⑦ ⑧ ⑨ ⑩
UNMOTIVATED / BORED	① ② ③ ④ ⑤ ⑥ ⑦ ⑧ ⑨ ⑩
SHORT ATTENTION	① ② ③ ④ ⑤ ⑥ ⑦ ⑧ ⑨ ⑩
FORGETFUL / CONFUSIONED	① ② ③ ④ ⑤ ⑥ ⑦ ⑧ ⑨ ⑩

HYPERACTIVITY

CONSTANTLY MOVING / TALKING	① ② ③ ④ ⑤ ⑥ ⑦ ⑧ ⑨ ⑩
STRUGGLING TO SIT STILL	① ② ③ ④ ⑤ ⑥ ⑦ ⑧ ⑨ ⑩
TOUCHING THINGS REPEATEDLY	① ② ③ ④ ⑤ ⑥ ⑦ ⑧ ⑨ ⑩
DIFFICULT SLEEPING	① ② ③ ④ ⑤ ⑥ ⑦ ⑧ ⑨ ⑩

IMPULSIVITY

ACTING WITHOUT THINKING	① ② ③ ④ ⑤ ⑥ ⑦ ⑧ ⑨ ⑩
INTERRUPTING OTHERS	① ② ③ ④ ⑤ ⑥ ⑦ ⑧ ⑨ ⑩
EASILY FRUSTRATED	① ② ③ ④ ⑤ ⑥ ⑦ ⑧ ⑨ ⑩
UNABLE TO HOLD BACK EMOTIONS	① ② ③ ④ ⑤ ⑥ ⑦ ⑧ ⑨ ⑩

MEALS	MEDICATIONS

Water Tracker 🍶 🍶 🍶 🍶 🍶 🍶 🍶

NOTES

....
....

DAY GOALS

1 ....
2 ....
3 ....

DATE
WEEK
LOCATION
WEIGHT

Mood Tracker

BEHAVIOR

INATTENTION

SHORT ATTENTION	① ② ③ ④ ⑤ ⑥ ⑦ ⑧ ⑨ ⑩
UNMOTIVATED / BORED	① ② ③ ④ ⑤ ⑥ ⑦ ⑧ ⑨ ⑩
SHORT ATTENTION	① ② ③ ④ ⑤ ⑥ ⑦ ⑧ ⑨ ⑩
FORGETFUL / CONFUSIONED	① ② ③ ④ ⑤ ⑥ ⑦ ⑧ ⑨ ⑩

HYPERACTIVITY

CONSTANTLY MOVING / TALKING	① ② ③ ④ ⑤ ⑥ ⑦ ⑧ ⑨ ⑩
STRUGGLING TO SIT STILL	① ② ③ ④ ⑤ ⑥ ⑦ ⑧ ⑨ ⑩
TOUCHING THINGS REPEATEDLY	① ② ③ ④ ⑤ ⑥ ⑦ ⑧ ⑨ ⑩
DIFFICULT SLEEPING	① ② ③ ④ ⑤ ⑥ ⑦ ⑧ ⑨ ⑩

IMPULSIVITY

ACTING WITHOUT THINKING	① ② ③ ④ ⑤ ⑥ ⑦ ⑧ ⑨ ⑩
INTERRUPTING OTHERS	① ② ③ ④ ⑤ ⑥ ⑦ ⑧ ⑨ ⑩
EASILY FRUSTRATED	① ② ③ ④ ⑤ ⑥ ⑦ ⑧ ⑨ ⑩
UNABLE TO HOLD BACK EMOTIONS	① ② ③ ④ ⑤ ⑥ ⑦ ⑧ ⑨ ⑩

MEALS

MEDICATIONS

Water Tracker

NOTES

....
....

DAY GOALS

1 ....
2 ....
3 ....

DATE
WEEK
LOCATION
WEIGHT

Mood Tracker ☹ 😐 😖 🙁 😠 😃

BEHAVIOR

INATTENTION

SHORT ATTENTION	① ② ③ ④ ⑤ ⑥ ⑦ ⑧ ⑨ ⑩
UNMOTIVATED / BORED	① ② ③ ④ ⑤ ⑥ ⑦ ⑧ ⑨ ⑩
SHORT ATTENTION	① ② ③ ④ ⑤ ⑥ ⑦ ⑧ ⑨ ⑩
FORGETFUL / CONFUSIONED	① ② ③ ④ ⑤ ⑥ ⑦ ⑧ ⑨ ⑩

HYPERACTIVITY

CONSTANTLY MOVING / TALKING	① ② ③ ④ ⑤ ⑥ ⑦ ⑧ ⑨ ⑩
STRUGGLING TO SIT STILL	① ② ③ ④ ⑤ ⑥ ⑦ ⑧ ⑨ ⑩
TOUCHING THINGS REPEATEDLY	① ② ③ ④ ⑤ ⑥ ⑦ ⑧ ⑨ ⑩
DIFFICULT SLEEPING	① ② ③ ④ ⑤ ⑥ ⑦ ⑧ ⑨ ⑩

IMPULSIVITY

ACTING WITHOUT THINKING	① ② ③ ④ ⑤ ⑥ ⑦ ⑧ ⑨ ⑩
INTERRUPTING OTHERS	① ② ③ ④ ⑤ ⑥ ⑦ ⑧ ⑨ ⑩
EASILY FRUSTRATED	① ② ③ ④ ⑤ ⑥ ⑦ ⑧ ⑨ ⑩
UNABLE TO HOLD BACK EMOTIONS	① ② ③ ④ ⑤ ⑥ ⑦ ⑧ ⑨ ⑩

MEALS	MEDICATIONS

Water Tracker 🍶 🍶 🍶 🍶 🍶 🍶 🍶

NOTES

....
....

DAY GOALS

1 ....
2 ....
3 ....

DATE
WEEK
LOCATION
WEIGHT

Mood Tracker 😕 😐 😖 😢 😠 😃

BEHAVIOR

INATTENTION

SHORT ATTENTION	① ② ③ ④ ⑤ ⑥ ⑦ ⑧ ⑨ ⑩
UNMOTIVATED / BORED	① ② ③ ④ ⑤ ⑥ ⑦ ⑧ ⑨ ⑩
SHORT ATTENTION	① ② ③ ④ ⑤ ⑥ ⑦ ⑧ ⑨ ⑩
FORGETFUL / CONFUSIONED	① ② ③ ④ ⑤ ⑥ ⑦ ⑧ ⑨ ⑩

HYPERACTIVITY

CONSTANTLY MOVING / TALKING	① ② ③ ④ ⑤ ⑥ ⑦ ⑧ ⑨ ⑩
STRUGGLING TO SIT STILL	① ② ③ ④ ⑤ ⑥ ⑦ ⑧ ⑨ ⑩
TOUCHING THINGS REPEATEDLY	① ② ③ ④ ⑤ ⑥ ⑦ ⑧ ⑨ ⑩
DIFFICULT SLEEPING	① ② ③ ④ ⑤ ⑥ ⑦ ⑧ ⑨ ⑩

IMPULSIVITY

ACTING WITHOUT THINKING	① ② ③ ④ ⑤ ⑥ ⑦ ⑧ ⑨ ⑩
INTERRUPTING OTHERS	① ② ③ ④ ⑤ ⑥ ⑦ ⑧ ⑨ ⑩
EASILY FRUSTRATED	① ② ③ ④ ⑤ ⑥ ⑦ ⑧ ⑨ ⑩
UNABLE TO HOLD BACK EMOTIONS	① ② ③ ④ ⑤ ⑥ ⑦ ⑧ ⑨ ⑩

MEALS

MEDICATIONS

Water Tracker 🍼 🍼 🍼 🍼 🍼 🍼 🍼

NOTES

....
....

DAY GOALS

1 ....
2 ....
3 ....

DATE ....
WEEK ....
LOCATION ....
WEIGHT ....

Mood Tracker ☹ 😐 >< 😢 😠 😀

BEHAVIOR

INATTENTION

SHORT ATTENTION	① ② ③ ④ ⑤ ⑥ ⑦ ⑧ ⑨ ⑩
UNMOTIVATED / BORED	① ② ③ ④ ⑤ ⑥ ⑦ ⑧ ⑨ ⑩
SHORT ATTENTION	① ② ③ ④ ⑤ ⑥ ⑦ ⑧ ⑨ ⑩
FORGETFUL / CONFUSIONED	① ② ③ ④ ⑤ ⑥ ⑦ ⑧ ⑨ ⑩

HYPERACTIVITY

CONSTANTLY MOVING / TALKING	① ② ③ ④ ⑤ ⑥ ⑦ ⑧ ⑨ ⑩
STRUGGLING TO SIT STILL	① ② ③ ④ ⑤ ⑥ ⑦ ⑧ ⑨ ⑩
TOUCHING THINGS REPEATEDLY	① ② ③ ④ ⑤ ⑥ ⑦ ⑧ ⑨ ⑩
DIFFICULT SLEEPING	① ② ③ ④ ⑤ ⑥ ⑦ ⑧ ⑨ ⑩

IMPULSIVITY

ACTING WITHOUT THINKING	① ② ③ ④ ⑤ ⑥ ⑦ ⑧ ⑨ ⑩
INTERRUPTING OTHERS	① ② ③ ④ ⑤ ⑥ ⑦ ⑧ ⑨ ⑩
EASILY FRUSTRATED	① ② ③ ④ ⑤ ⑥ ⑦ ⑧ ⑨ ⑩
UNABLE TO HOLD BACK EMOTIONS	① ② ③ ④ ⑤ ⑥ ⑦ ⑧ ⑨ ⑩

MEALS

MEDICATIONS

Water Tracker 🍼 🍼 🍼 🍼 🍼 🍼 🍼

NOTES

....
....

DAY GOALS

1 ....
2 ....
3 ....

DATE

WEEK

LOCATION

WEIGHT

Mood Tracker ☹ 😐 😖 😢 😠 😃

BEHAVIOR

INATTENTION

SHORT ATTENTION	① ② ③ ④ ⑤ ⑥ ⑦ ⑧ ⑨ ⑩
UNMOTIVATED / BORED	① ② ③ ④ ⑤ ⑥ ⑦ ⑧ ⑨ ⑩
SHORT ATTENTION	① ② ③ ④ ⑤ ⑥ ⑦ ⑧ ⑨ ⑩
FORGETFUL / CONFUSIONED	① ② ③ ④ ⑤ ⑥ ⑦ ⑧ ⑨ ⑩

HYPERACTIVITY

CONSTANTLY MOVING / TALKING	① ② ③ ④ ⑤ ⑥ ⑦ ⑧ ⑨ ⑩
STRUGGLING TO SIT STILL	① ② ③ ④ ⑤ ⑥ ⑦ ⑧ ⑨ ⑩
TOUCHING THINGS REPEATEDLY	① ② ③ ④ ⑤ ⑥ ⑦ ⑧ ⑨ ⑩
DIFFICULT SLEEPING	① ② ③ ④ ⑤ ⑥ ⑦ ⑧ ⑨ ⑩

IMPULSIVITY

ACTING WITHOUT THINKING	① ② ③ ④ ⑤ ⑥ ⑦ ⑧ ⑨ ⑩
INTERRUPTING OTHERS	① ② ③ ④ ⑤ ⑥ ⑦ ⑧ ⑨ ⑩
EASILY FRUSTRATED	① ② ③ ④ ⑤ ⑥ ⑦ ⑧ ⑨ ⑩
UNABLE TO HOLD BACK EMOTIONS	① ② ③ ④ ⑤ ⑥ ⑦ ⑧ ⑨ ⑩

MEALS	MEDICATIONS

Water Tracker 🍼 🍼 🍼 🍼 🍼 🍼 🍼

NOTES

....
....

DAY GOALS

1 ....
2 ....
3 ....

DATE
WEEK
LOCATION
WEIGHT

Mood Tracker ☹ 😐 😖 😢 😠 😃

BEHAVIOR

INATTENTION

Behavior	Rating
SHORT ATTENTION	① ② ③ ④ ⑤ ⑥ ⑦ ⑧ ⑨ ⑩
UNMOTIVATED / BORED	① ② ③ ④ ⑤ ⑥ ⑦ ⑧ ⑨ ⑩
SHORT ATTENTION	① ② ③ ④ ⑤ ⑥ ⑦ ⑧ ⑨ ⑩
FORGETFUL / CONFUSIONED	① ② ③ ④ ⑤ ⑥ ⑦ ⑧ ⑨ ⑩

HYPERACTIVITY

Behavior	Rating
CONSTANTLY MOVING / TALKING	① ② ③ ④ ⑤ ⑥ ⑦ ⑧ ⑨ ⑩
STRUGGLING TO SIT STILL	① ② ③ ④ ⑤ ⑥ ⑦ ⑧ ⑨ ⑩
TOUCHING THINGS REPEATEDLY	① ② ③ ④ ⑤ ⑥ ⑦ ⑧ ⑨ ⑩
DIFFICULT SLEEPING	① ② ③ ④ ⑤ ⑥ ⑦ ⑧ ⑨ ⑩

IMPULSIVITY

Behavior	Rating
ACTING WITHOUT THINKING	① ② ③ ④ ⑤ ⑥ ⑦ ⑧ ⑨ ⑩
INTERRUPTING OTHERS	① ② ③ ④ ⑤ ⑥ ⑦ ⑧ ⑨ ⑩
EASILY FRUSTRATED	① ② ③ ④ ⑤ ⑥ ⑦ ⑧ ⑨ ⑩
UNABLE TO HOLD BACK EMOTIONS	① ② ③ ④ ⑤ ⑥ ⑦ ⑧ ⑨ ⑩

MEALS

MEDICATIONS

Water Tracker 🍶 🍶 🍶 🍶 🍶 🍶 🍶 🍶

NOTES

....
....

DAY GOALS	
1	DATE
2	WEEK
3	LOCATION
	WEIGHT

Mood Tracker ☹ 😐 😖 😢 😠 😃

BEHAVIOR

INATTENTION

SHORT ATTENTION	① ② ③ ④ ⑤ ⑥ ⑦ ⑧ ⑨ ⑩
UNMOTIVATED / BORED	① ② ③ ④ ⑤ ⑥ ⑦ ⑧ ⑨ ⑩
SHORT ATTENTION	① ② ③ ④ ⑤ ⑥ ⑦ ⑧ ⑨ ⑩
FORGETFUL / CONFUSIONED	① ② ③ ④ ⑤ ⑥ ⑦ ⑧ ⑨ ⑩

HYPERACTIVITY

CONSTANTLY MOVING / TALKING	① ② ③ ④ ⑤ ⑥ ⑦ ⑧ ⑨ ⑩
STRUGGLING TO SIT STILL	① ② ③ ④ ⑤ ⑥ ⑦ ⑧ ⑨ ⑩
TOUCHING THINGS REPEATEDLY	① ② ③ ④ ⑤ ⑥ ⑦ ⑧ ⑨ ⑩
DIFFICULT SLEEPING	① ② ③ ④ ⑤ ⑥ ⑦ ⑧ ⑨ ⑩

IMPULSIVITY

ACTING WITHOUT THINKING	① ② ③ ④ ⑤ ⑥ ⑦ ⑧ ⑨ ⑩
INTERRUPTING OTHERS	① ② ③ ④ ⑤ ⑥ ⑦ ⑧ ⑨ ⑩
EASILY FRUSTRATED	① ② ③ ④ ⑤ ⑥ ⑦ ⑧ ⑨ ⑩
UNABLE TO HOLD BACK EMOTIONS	① ② ③ ④ ⑤ ⑥ ⑦ ⑧ ⑨ ⑩

MEALS	MEDICATIONS

Water Tracker 🍼 🍼 🍼 🍼 🍼 🍼 🍼

NOTES

....
....

DAY GOALS	
1	
2	
3	

DATE
WEEK
LOCATION
WEIGHT

Mood Tracker ☹ 😐 😖 😢 😠 😃

BEHAVIOR

INATTENTION

SHORT ATTENTION	① ② ③ ④ ⑤ ⑥ ⑦ ⑧ ⑨ ⑩
UNMOTIVATED / BORED	① ② ③ ④ ⑤ ⑥ ⑦ ⑧ ⑨ ⑩
SHORT ATTENTION	① ② ③ ④ ⑤ ⑥ ⑦ ⑧ ⑨ ⑩
FORGETFUL / CONFUSIONED	① ② ③ ④ ⑤ ⑥ ⑦ ⑧ ⑨ ⑩

HYPERACTIVITY

CONSTANTLY MOVING / TALKING	① ② ③ ④ ⑤ ⑥ ⑦ ⑧ ⑨ ⑩
STRUGGLING TO SIT STILL	① ② ③ ④ ⑤ ⑥ ⑦ ⑧ ⑨ ⑩
TOUCHING THINGS REPEATEDLY	① ② ③ ④ ⑤ ⑥ ⑦ ⑧ ⑨ ⑩
DIFFICULT SLEEPING	① ② ③ ④ ⑤ ⑥ ⑦ ⑧ ⑨ ⑩

IMPULSIVITY

ACTING WITHOUT THINKING	① ② ③ ④ ⑤ ⑥ ⑦ ⑧ ⑨ ⑩
INTERRUPTING OTHERS	① ② ③ ④ ⑤ ⑥ ⑦ ⑧ ⑨ ⑩
EASILY FRUSTRATED	① ② ③ ④ ⑤ ⑥ ⑦ ⑧ ⑨ ⑩
UNABLE TO HOLD BACK EMOTIONS	① ② ③ ④ ⑤ ⑥ ⑦ ⑧ ⑨ ⑩

MEALS	MEDICATIONS

Water Tracker 🍼 🍼 🍼 🍼 🍼 🍼 🍼 🍼

NOTES

....
....

DAY GOALS

1 ....
2 ....
3 ....

DATE

WEEK

LOCATION

WEIGHT

Mood Tracker

BEHAVIOR

INATTENTION

SHORT ATTENTION	① ② ③ ④ ⑤ ⑥ ⑦ ⑧ ⑨ ⑩
UNMOTIVATED / BORED	① ② ③ ④ ⑤ ⑥ ⑦ ⑧ ⑨ ⑩
SHORT ATTENTION	① ② ③ ④ ⑤ ⑥ ⑦ ⑧ ⑨ ⑩
FORGETFUL / CONFUSIONED	① ② ③ ④ ⑤ ⑥ ⑦ ⑧ ⑨ ⑩

HYPERACTIVITY

CONSTANTLY MOVING / TALKING	① ② ③ ④ ⑤ ⑥ ⑦ ⑧ ⑨ ⑩
STRUGGLING TO SIT STILL	① ② ③ ④ ⑤ ⑥ ⑦ ⑧ ⑨ ⑩
TOUCHING THINGS REPEATEDLY	① ② ③ ④ ⑤ ⑥ ⑦ ⑧ ⑨ ⑩
DIFFICULT SLEEPING	① ② ③ ④ ⑤ ⑥ ⑦ ⑧ ⑨ ⑩

IMPULSIVITY

ACTING WITHOUT THINKING	① ② ③ ④ ⑤ ⑥ ⑦ ⑧ ⑨ ⑩
INTERRUPTING OTHERS	① ② ③ ④ ⑤ ⑥ ⑦ ⑧ ⑨ ⑩
EASILY FRUSTRATED	① ② ③ ④ ⑤ ⑥ ⑦ ⑧ ⑨ ⑩
UNABLE TO HOLD BACK EMOTIONS	① ② ③ ④ ⑤ ⑥ ⑦ ⑧ ⑨ ⑩

MEALS

MEDICATIONS

Water Tracker

NOTES

....
....

DAY GOALS	
1	
2	
3	

DATE
WEEK
LOCATION
WEIGHT

Mood Tracker

BEHAVIOR

INATTENTION

SHORT ATTENTION	① ② ③ ④ ⑤ ⑥ ⑦ ⑧ ⑨ ⑩
UNMOTIVATED / BORED	① ② ③ ④ ⑤ ⑥ ⑦ ⑧ ⑨ ⑩
SHORT ATTENTION	① ② ③ ④ ⑤ ⑥ ⑦ ⑧ ⑨ ⑩
FORGETFUL / CONFUSIONED	① ② ③ ④ ⑤ ⑥ ⑦ ⑧ ⑨ ⑩

HYPERACTIVITY

CONSTANTLY MOVING / TALKING	① ② ③ ④ ⑤ ⑥ ⑦ ⑧ ⑨ ⑩
STRUGGLING TO SIT STILL	① ② ③ ④ ⑤ ⑥ ⑦ ⑧ ⑨ ⑩
TOUCHING THINGS REPEATEDLY	① ② ③ ④ ⑤ ⑥ ⑦ ⑧ ⑨ ⑩
DIFFICULT SLEEPING	① ② ③ ④ ⑤ ⑥ ⑦ ⑧ ⑨ ⑩

IMPULSIVITY

ACTING WITHOUT THINKING	① ② ③ ④ ⑤ ⑥ ⑦ ⑧ ⑨ ⑩
INTERRUPTING OTHERS	① ② ③ ④ ⑤ ⑥ ⑦ ⑧ ⑨ ⑩
EASILY FRUSTRATED	① ② ③ ④ ⑤ ⑥ ⑦ ⑧ ⑨ ⑩
UNABLE TO HOLD BACK EMOTIONS	① ② ③ ④ ⑤ ⑥ ⑦ ⑧ ⑨ ⑩

MEALS

MEDICATIONS

Water Tracker

NOTES

....
....

DAY GOALS

1 ....
2 ....
3 ....

DATE

WEEK

LOCATION

WEIGHT

Mood Tracker 😟 😐 😖 😢 😠 😃

BEHAVIOR

INATTENTION

SHORT ATTENTION	① ② ③ ④ ⑤ ⑥ ⑦ ⑧ ⑨ ⑩
UNMOTIVATED / BORED	① ② ③ ④ ⑤ ⑥ ⑦ ⑧ ⑨ ⑩
SHORT ATTENTION	① ② ③ ④ ⑤ ⑥ ⑦ ⑧ ⑨ ⑩
FORGETFUL / CONFUSIONED	① ② ③ ④ ⑤ ⑥ ⑦ ⑧ ⑨ ⑩

HYPERACTIVITY

CONSTANTLY MOVING / TALKING	① ② ③ ④ ⑤ ⑥ ⑦ ⑧ ⑨ ⑩
STRUGGLING TO SIT STILL	① ② ③ ④ ⑤ ⑥ ⑦ ⑧ ⑨ ⑩
TOUCHING THINGS REPEATEDLY	① ② ③ ④ ⑤ ⑥ ⑦ ⑧ ⑨ ⑩
DIFFICULT SLEEPING	① ② ③ ④ ⑤ ⑥ ⑦ ⑧ ⑨ ⑩

IMPULSIVITY

ACTING WITHOUT THINKING	① ② ③ ④ ⑤ ⑥ ⑦ ⑧ ⑨ ⑩
INTERRUPTING OTHERS	① ② ③ ④ ⑤ ⑥ ⑦ ⑧ ⑨ ⑩
EASILY FRUSTRATED	① ② ③ ④ ⑤ ⑥ ⑦ ⑧ ⑨ ⑩
UNABLE TO HOLD BACK EMOTIONS	① ② ③ ④ ⑤ ⑥ ⑦ ⑧ ⑨ ⑩

MEALS

MEDICATIONS

Water Tracker 🍼 🍼 🍼 🍼 🍼 🍼 🍼

NOTES

....
....

DAY GOALS

1 ....
2 ....
3 ....

DATE
WEEK
LOCATION
WEIGHT

Mood Tracker ☹ 😐 🤢 😢 😠 😃

BEHAVIOR

INATTENTION

SHORT ATTENTION	① ② ③ ④ ⑤ ⑥ ⑦ ⑧ ⑨ ⑩
UNMOTIVATED / BORED	① ② ③ ④ ⑤ ⑥ ⑦ ⑧ ⑨ ⑩
SHORT ATTENTION	① ② ③ ④ ⑤ ⑥ ⑦ ⑧ ⑨ ⑩
FORGETFUL / CONFUSIONED	① ② ③ ④ ⑤ ⑥ ⑦ ⑧ ⑨ ⑩

HYPERACTIVITY

CONSTANTLY MOVING / TALKING	① ② ③ ④ ⑤ ⑥ ⑦ ⑧ ⑨ ⑩
STRUGGLING TO SIT STILL	① ② ③ ④ ⑤ ⑥ ⑦ ⑧ ⑨ ⑩
TOUCHING THINGS REPEATEDLY	① ② ③ ④ ⑤ ⑥ ⑦ ⑧ ⑨ ⑩
DIFFICULT SLEEPING	① ② ③ ④ ⑤ ⑥ ⑦ ⑧ ⑨ ⑩

IMPULSIVITY

ACTING WITHOUT THINKING	① ② ③ ④ ⑤ ⑥ ⑦ ⑧ ⑨ ⑩
INTERRUPTING OTHERS	① ② ③ ④ ⑤ ⑥ ⑦ ⑧ ⑨ ⑩
EASILY FRUSTRATED	① ② ③ ④ ⑤ ⑥ ⑦ ⑧ ⑨ ⑩
UNABLE TO HOLD BACK EMOTIONS	① ② ③ ④ ⑤ ⑥ ⑦ ⑧ ⑨ ⑩

MEALS

MEDICATIONS

Water Tracker 🍼 🍼 🍼 🍼 🍼 🍼 🍼

NOTES

....
....

DAY GOALS

1 ....
2 ....
3 ....

DATE
WEEK
LOCATION
WEIGHT

Mood Tracker

BEHAVIOR

INATTENTION

SHORT ATTENTION	① ② ③ ④ ⑤ ⑥ ⑦ ⑧ ⑨ ⑩
UNMOTIVATED / BORED	① ② ③ ④ ⑤ ⑥ ⑦ ⑧ ⑨ ⑩
SHORT ATTENTION	① ② ③ ④ ⑤ ⑥ ⑦ ⑧ ⑨ ⑩
FORGETFUL / CONFUSIONED	① ② ③ ④ ⑤ ⑥ ⑦ ⑧ ⑨ ⑩

HYPERACTIVITY

CONSTANTLY MOVING / TALKING	① ② ③ ④ ⑤ ⑥ ⑦ ⑧ ⑨ ⑩
STRUGGLING TO SIT STILL	① ② ③ ④ ⑤ ⑥ ⑦ ⑧ ⑨ ⑩
TOUCHING THINGS REPEATEDLY	① ② ③ ④ ⑤ ⑥ ⑦ ⑧ ⑨ ⑩
DIFFICULT SLEEPING	① ② ③ ④ ⑤ ⑥ ⑦ ⑧ ⑨ ⑩

IMPULSIVITY

ACTING WITHOUT THINKING	① ② ③ ④ ⑤ ⑥ ⑦ ⑧ ⑨ ⑩
INTERRUPTING OTHERS	① ② ③ ④ ⑤ ⑥ ⑦ ⑧ ⑨ ⑩
EASILY FRUSTRATED	① ② ③ ④ ⑤ ⑥ ⑦ ⑧ ⑨ ⑩
UNABLE TO HOLD BACK EMOTIONS	① ② ③ ④ ⑤ ⑥ ⑦ ⑧ ⑨ ⑩

MEALS

MEDICATIONS

Water Tracker

NOTES

....
....

DAY GOALS		DATE	
1		WEEK	
2		LOCATION	
3		WEIGHT	

Mood Tracker 😟 😐 >< 😢 😠 😃

BEHAVIOR

INATTENTION

SHORT ATTENTION	① ② ③ ④ ⑤ ⑥ ⑦ ⑧ ⑨ ⑩
UNMOTIVATED / BORED	① ② ③ ④ ⑤ ⑥ ⑦ ⑧ ⑨ ⑩
SHORT ATTENTION	① ② ③ ④ ⑤ ⑥ ⑦ ⑧ ⑨ ⑩
FORGETFUL / CONFUSIONED	① ② ③ ④ ⑤ ⑥ ⑦ ⑧ ⑨ ⑩

HYPERACTIVITY

CONSTANTLY MOVING / TALKING	① ② ③ ④ ⑤ ⑥ ⑦ ⑧ ⑨ ⑩
STRUGGLING TO SIT STILL	① ② ③ ④ ⑤ ⑥ ⑦ ⑧ ⑨ ⑩
TOUCHING THINGS REPEATEDLY	① ② ③ ④ ⑤ ⑥ ⑦ ⑧ ⑨ ⑩
DIFFICULT SLEEPING	① ② ③ ④ ⑤ ⑥ ⑦ ⑧ ⑨ ⑩

IMPULSIVITY

ACTING WITHOUT THINKING	① ② ③ ④ ⑤ ⑥ ⑦ ⑧ ⑨ ⑩
INTERRUPTING OTHERS	① ② ③ ④ ⑤ ⑥ ⑦ ⑧ ⑨ ⑩
EASILY FRUSTRATED	① ② ③ ④ ⑤ ⑥ ⑦ ⑧ ⑨ ⑩
UNABLE TO HOLD BACK EMOTIONS	① ② ③ ④ ⑤ ⑥ ⑦ ⑧ ⑨ ⑩

MEALS	MEDICATIONS

Water Tracker 🍶 🍶 🍶 🍶 🍶 🍶 🍶

NOTES

....
....

DAY GOALS

1 ....
2 ....
3 ....

DATE
WEEK
LOCATION
WEIGHT

Mood Tracker ☹ 😐 😖 😢 😠 😃

BEHAVIOR

INATTENTION

SHORT ATTENTION	① ② ③ ④ ⑤ ⑥ ⑦ ⑧ ⑨ ⑩
UNMOTIVATED / BORED	① ② ③ ④ ⑤ ⑥ ⑦ ⑧ ⑨ ⑩
SHORT ATTENTION	① ② ③ ④ ⑤ ⑥ ⑦ ⑧ ⑨ ⑩
FORGETFUL / CONFUSIONED	① ② ③ ④ ⑤ ⑥ ⑦ ⑧ ⑨ ⑩

HYPERACTIVITY

CONSTANTLY MOVING / TALKING	① ② ③ ④ ⑤ ⑥ ⑦ ⑧ ⑨ ⑩
STRUGGLING TO SIT STILL	① ② ③ ④ ⑤ ⑥ ⑦ ⑧ ⑨ ⑩
TOUCHING THINGS REPEATEDLY	① ② ③ ④ ⑤ ⑥ ⑦ ⑧ ⑨ ⑩
DIFFICULT SLEEPING	① ② ③ ④ ⑤ ⑥ ⑦ ⑧ ⑨ ⑩

IMPULSIVITY

ACTING WITHOUT THINKING	① ② ③ ④ ⑤ ⑥ ⑦ ⑧ ⑨ ⑩
INTERRUPTING OTHERS	① ② ③ ④ ⑤ ⑥ ⑦ ⑧ ⑨ ⑩
EASILY FRUSTRATED	① ② ③ ④ ⑤ ⑥ ⑦ ⑧ ⑨ ⑩
UNABLE TO HOLD BACK EMOTIONS	① ② ③ ④ ⑤ ⑥ ⑦ ⑧ ⑨ ⑩

MEALS	MEDICATIONS

Water Tracker 🍼 🍼 🍼 🍼 🍼 🍼 🍼

NOTES

....
....

DAY GOALS	DATE
1	WEEK
2	LOCATION
3	WEIGHT

Mood Tracker 😕 😐 😖 😢 😠 😃

BEHAVIOR

INATTENTION

SHORT ATTENTION	① ② ③ ④ ⑤ ⑥ ⑦ ⑧ ⑨ ⑩
UNMOTIVATED / BORED	① ② ③ ④ ⑤ ⑥ ⑦ ⑧ ⑨ ⑩
SHORT ATTENTION	① ② ③ ④ ⑤ ⑥ ⑦ ⑧ ⑨ ⑩
FORGETFUL / CONFUSIONED	① ② ③ ④ ⑤ ⑥ ⑦ ⑧ ⑨ ⑩

HYPERACTIVITY

CONSTANTLY MOVING / TALKING	① ② ③ ④ ⑤ ⑥ ⑦ ⑧ ⑨ ⑩
STRUGGLING TO SIT STILL	① ② ③ ④ ⑤ ⑥ ⑦ ⑧ ⑨ ⑩
TOUCHING THINGS REPEATEDLY	① ② ③ ④ ⑤ ⑥ ⑦ ⑧ ⑨ ⑩
DIFFICULT SLEEPING	① ② ③ ④ ⑤ ⑥ ⑦ ⑧ ⑨ ⑩

IMPULSIVITY

ACTING WITHOUT THINKING	① ② ③ ④ ⑤ ⑥ ⑦ ⑧ ⑨ ⑩
INTERRUPTING OTHERS	① ② ③ ④ ⑤ ⑥ ⑦ ⑧ ⑨ ⑩
EASILY FRUSTRATED	① ② ③ ④ ⑤ ⑥ ⑦ ⑧ ⑨ ⑩
UNABLE TO HOLD BACK EMOTIONS	① ② ③ ④ ⑤ ⑥ ⑦ ⑧ ⑨ ⑩

MEALS	MEDICATIONS

Water Tracker 🍶 🍶 🍶 🍶 🍶 🍶 🍶

NOTES

....
....

DAY GOALS

1 ....
2 ....
3 ....

DATE

WEEK

LOCATION

WEIGHT

Mood Tracker   ☹ 😐 😖 😢 😠 😀

BEHAVIOR

INATTENTION

SHORT ATTENTION	① ② ③ ④ ⑤ ⑥ ⑦ ⑧ ⑨ ⑩
UNMOTIVATED / BORED	① ② ③ ④ ⑤ ⑥ ⑦ ⑧ ⑨ ⑩
SHORT ATTENTION	① ② ③ ④ ⑤ ⑥ ⑦ ⑧ ⑨ ⑩
FORGETFUL / CONFUSIONED	① ② ③ ④ ⑤ ⑥ ⑦ ⑧ ⑨ ⑩

HYPERACTIVITY

CONSTANTLY MOVING / TALKING	① ② ③ ④ ⑤ ⑥ ⑦ ⑧ ⑨ ⑩
STRUGGLING TO SIT STILL	① ② ③ ④ ⑤ ⑥ ⑦ ⑧ ⑨ ⑩
TOUCHING THINGS REPEATEDLY	① ② ③ ④ ⑤ ⑥ ⑦ ⑧ ⑨ ⑩
DIFFICULT SLEEPING	① ② ③ ④ ⑤ ⑥ ⑦ ⑧ ⑨ ⑩

IMPULSIVITY

ACTING WITHOUT THINKING	① ② ③ ④ ⑤ ⑥ ⑦ ⑧ ⑨ ⑩
INTERRUPTING OTHERS	① ② ③ ④ ⑤ ⑥ ⑦ ⑧ ⑨ ⑩
EASILY FRUSTRATED	① ② ③ ④ ⑤ ⑥ ⑦ ⑧ ⑨ ⑩
UNABLE TO HOLD BACK EMOTIONS	① ② ③ ④ ⑤ ⑥ ⑦ ⑧ ⑨ ⑩

MEALS

MEDICATIONS

Water Tracker   🍼 🍼 🍼 🍼 🍼 🍼 🍼

NOTES

....
....

DAY GOALS

1 ....
2 ....
3 ....

DATE
WEEK
LOCATION
WEIGHT

Mood Tracker ☹ 😐 😖 😢 😠 😃

BEHAVIOR

INATTENTION

SHORT ATTENTION	① ② ③ ④ ⑤ ⑥ ⑦ ⑧ ⑨ ⑩
UNMOTIVATED / BORED	① ② ③ ④ ⑤ ⑥ ⑦ ⑧ ⑨ ⑩
SHORT ATTENTION	① ② ③ ④ ⑤ ⑥ ⑦ ⑧ ⑨ ⑩
FORGETFUL / CONFUSIONED	① ② ③ ④ ⑤ ⑥ ⑦ ⑧ ⑨ ⑩

HYPERACTIVITY

CONSTANTLY MOVING / TALKING	① ② ③ ④ ⑤ ⑥ ⑦ ⑧ ⑨ ⑩
STRUGGLING TO SIT STILL	① ② ③ ④ ⑤ ⑥ ⑦ ⑧ ⑨ ⑩
TOUCHING THINGS REPEATEDLY	① ② ③ ④ ⑤ ⑥ ⑦ ⑧ ⑨ ⑩
DIFFICULT SLEEPING	① ② ③ ④ ⑤ ⑥ ⑦ ⑧ ⑨ ⑩

IMPULSIVITY

ACTING WITHOUT THINKING	① ② ③ ④ ⑤ ⑥ ⑦ ⑧ ⑨ ⑩
INTERRUPTING OTHERS	① ② ③ ④ ⑤ ⑥ ⑦ ⑧ ⑨ ⑩
EASILY FRUSTRATED	① ② ③ ④ ⑤ ⑥ ⑦ ⑧ ⑨ ⑩
UNABLE TO HOLD BACK EMOTIONS	① ② ③ ④ ⑤ ⑥ ⑦ ⑧ ⑨ ⑩

MEALS

MEDICATIONS

Water Tracker 🍼 🍼 🍼 🍼 🍼 🍼 🍼

NOTES

....
....

DAY GOALS	
1	DATE
2	WEEK
3	LOCATION
	WEIGHT

Mood Tracker   😐 😑 😖 😢 😠 😃

BEHAVIOR

INATTENTION

SHORT ATTENTION	① ② ③ ④ ⑤ ⑥ ⑦ ⑧ ⑨ ⑩
UNMOTIVATED / BORED	① ② ③ ④ ⑤ ⑥ ⑦ ⑧ ⑨ ⑩
SHORT ATTENTION	① ② ③ ④ ⑤ ⑥ ⑦ ⑧ ⑨ ⑩
FORGETFUL / CONFUSIONED	① ② ③ ④ ⑤ ⑥ ⑦ ⑧ ⑨ ⑩

HYPERACTIVITY

CONSTANTLY MOVING / TALKING	① ② ③ ④ ⑤ ⑥ ⑦ ⑧ ⑨ ⑩
STRUGGLING TO SIT STILL	① ② ③ ④ ⑤ ⑥ ⑦ ⑧ ⑨ ⑩
TOUCHING THINGS REPEATEDLY	① ② ③ ④ ⑤ ⑥ ⑦ ⑧ ⑨ ⑩
DIFFICULT SLEEPING	① ② ③ ④ ⑤ ⑥ ⑦ ⑧ ⑨ ⑩

IMPULSIVITY

ACTING WITHOUT THINKING	① ② ③ ④ ⑤ ⑥ ⑦ ⑧ ⑨ ⑩
INTERRUPTING OTHERS	① ② ③ ④ ⑤ ⑥ ⑦ ⑧ ⑨ ⑩
EASILY FRUSTRATED	① ② ③ ④ ⑤ ⑥ ⑦ ⑧ ⑨ ⑩
UNABLE TO HOLD BACK EMOTIONS	① ② ③ ④ ⑤ ⑥ ⑦ ⑧ ⑨ ⑩

MEALS	MEDICATIONS

Water Tracker 🍼 🍼 🍼 🍼 🍼 🍼 🍼

NOTES

....
....

DAY GOALS	
1	
2	
3	

DATE
WEEK
LOCATION
WEIGHT

Mood Tracker   😟 😐 😖 😢 😠 😃

BEHAVIOR

INATTENTION

SHORT ATTENTION	① ② ③ ④ ⑤ ⑥ ⑦ ⑧ ⑨ ⑩
UNMOTIVATED / BORED	① ② ③ ④ ⑤ ⑥ ⑦ ⑧ ⑨ ⑩
SHORT ATTENTION	① ② ③ ④ ⑤ ⑥ ⑦ ⑧ ⑨ ⑩
FORGETFUL / CONFUSIONED	① ② ③ ④ ⑤ ⑥ ⑦ ⑧ ⑨ ⑩

HYPERACTIVITY

CONSTANTLY MOVING / TALKING	① ② ③ ④ ⑤ ⑥ ⑦ ⑧ ⑨ ⑩
STRUGGLING TO SIT STILL	① ② ③ ④ ⑤ ⑥ ⑦ ⑧ ⑨ ⑩
TOUCHING THINGS REPEATEDLY	① ② ③ ④ ⑤ ⑥ ⑦ ⑧ ⑨ ⑩
DIFFICULT SLEEPING	① ② ③ ④ ⑤ ⑥ ⑦ ⑧ ⑨ ⑩

IMPULSIVITY

ACTING WITHOUT THINKING	① ② ③ ④ ⑤ ⑥ ⑦ ⑧ ⑨ ⑩
INTERRUPTING OTHERS	① ② ③ ④ ⑤ ⑥ ⑦ ⑧ ⑨ ⑩
EASILY FRUSTRATED	① ② ③ ④ ⑤ ⑥ ⑦ ⑧ ⑨ ⑩
UNABLE TO HOLD BACK EMOTIONS	① ② ③ ④ ⑤ ⑥ ⑦ ⑧ ⑨ ⑩

MEALS	MEDICATIONS

Water Tracker 🍼 🍼 🍼 🍼 🍼 🍼 🍼

NOTES

....
....

DAY GOALS

1 ....
2 ....
3 ....

DATE
WEEK
LOCATION
WEIGHT

Mood Tracker 😟 😐 😖 😢 😠 😀

BEHAVIOR

INATTENTION

SHORT ATTENTION	① ② ③ ④ ⑤ ⑥ ⑦ ⑧ ⑨ ⑩
UNMOTIVATED / BORED	① ② ③ ④ ⑤ ⑥ ⑦ ⑧ ⑨ ⑩
SHORT ATTENTION	① ② ③ ④ ⑤ ⑥ ⑦ ⑧ ⑨ ⑩
FORGETFUL / CONFUSIONED	① ② ③ ④ ⑤ ⑥ ⑦ ⑧ ⑨ ⑩

HYPERACTIVITY

CONSTANTLY MOVING / TALKING	① ② ③ ④ ⑤ ⑥ ⑦ ⑧ ⑨ ⑩
STRUGGLING TO SIT STILL	① ② ③ ④ ⑤ ⑥ ⑦ ⑧ ⑨ ⑩
TOUCHING THINGS REPEATEDLY	① ② ③ ④ ⑤ ⑥ ⑦ ⑧ ⑨ ⑩
DIFFICULT SLEEPING	① ② ③ ④ ⑤ ⑥ ⑦ ⑧ ⑨ ⑩

IMPULSIVITY

ACTING WITHOUT THINKING	① ② ③ ④ ⑤ ⑥ ⑦ ⑧ ⑨ ⑩
INTERRUPTING OTHERS	① ② ③ ④ ⑤ ⑥ ⑦ ⑧ ⑨ ⑩
EASILY FRUSTRATED	① ② ③ ④ ⑤ ⑥ ⑦ ⑧ ⑨ ⑩
UNABLE TO HOLD BACK EMOTIONS	① ② ③ ④ ⑤ ⑥ ⑦ ⑧ ⑨ ⑩

MEALS

MEDICATIONS

Water Tracker 🍼 🍼 🍼 🍼 🍼 🍼 🍼

NOTES

....
....

DAY GOALS

1 ....
2 ....
3 ....

DATE
WEEK
LOCATION
WEIGHT

Mood Tracker

BEHAVIOR

INATTENTION

SHORT ATTENTION	① ② ③ ④ ⑤ ⑥ ⑦ ⑧ ⑨ ⑩
UNMOTIVATED / BORED	① ② ③ ④ ⑤ ⑥ ⑦ ⑧ ⑨ ⑩
SHORT ATTENTION	① ② ③ ④ ⑤ ⑥ ⑦ ⑧ ⑨ ⑩
FORGETFUL / CONFUSIONED	① ② ③ ④ ⑤ ⑥ ⑦ ⑧ ⑨ ⑩

HYPERACTIVITY

CONSTANTLY MOVING / TALKING	① ② ③ ④ ⑤ ⑥ ⑦ ⑧ ⑨ ⑩
STRUGGLING TO SIT STILL	① ② ③ ④ ⑤ ⑥ ⑦ ⑧ ⑨ ⑩
TOUCHING THINGS REPEATEDLY	① ② ③ ④ ⑤ ⑥ ⑦ ⑧ ⑨ ⑩
DIFFICULT SLEEPING	① ② ③ ④ ⑤ ⑥ ⑦ ⑧ ⑨ ⑩

IMPULSIVITY

ACTING WITHOUT THINKING	① ② ③ ④ ⑤ ⑥ ⑦ ⑧ ⑨ ⑩
INTERRUPTING OTHERS	① ② ③ ④ ⑤ ⑥ ⑦ ⑧ ⑨ ⑩
EASILY FRUSTRATED	① ② ③ ④ ⑤ ⑥ ⑦ ⑧ ⑨ ⑩
UNABLE TO HOLD BACK EMOTIONS	① ② ③ ④ ⑤ ⑥ ⑦ ⑧ ⑨ ⑩

MEALS

MEDICATIONS

Water Tracker

NOTES

....
....

DAY GOALS

1 ....
2 ....
3 ....

DATE
WEEK
LOCATION
WEIGHT

Mood Tracker 😟 😐 😣 😢 😠 😃

BEHAVIOR

INATTENTION

SHORT ATTENTION	① ② ③ ④ ⑤ ⑥ ⑦ ⑧ ⑨ ⑩
UNMOTIVATED / BORED	① ② ③ ④ ⑤ ⑥ ⑦ ⑧ ⑨ ⑩
SHORT ATTENTION	① ② ③ ④ ⑤ ⑥ ⑦ ⑧ ⑨ ⑩
FORGETFUL / CONFUSIONED	① ② ③ ④ ⑤ ⑥ ⑦ ⑧ ⑨ ⑩

HYPERACTIVITY

CONSTANTLY MOVING / TALKING	① ② ③ ④ ⑤ ⑥ ⑦ ⑧ ⑨ ⑩
STRUGGLING TO SIT STILL	① ② ③ ④ ⑤ ⑥ ⑦ ⑧ ⑨ ⑩
TOUCHING THINGS REPEATEDLY	① ② ③ ④ ⑤ ⑥ ⑦ ⑧ ⑨ ⑩
DIFFICULT SLEEPING	① ② ③ ④ ⑤ ⑥ ⑦ ⑧ ⑨ ⑩

IMPULSIVITY

ACTING WITHOUT THINKING	① ② ③ ④ ⑤ ⑥ ⑦ ⑧ ⑨ ⑩
INTERRUPTING OTHERS	① ② ③ ④ ⑤ ⑥ ⑦ ⑧ ⑨ ⑩
EASILY FRUSTRATED	① ② ③ ④ ⑤ ⑥ ⑦ ⑧ ⑨ ⑩
UNABLE TO HOLD BACK EMOTIONS	① ② ③ ④ ⑤ ⑥ ⑦ ⑧ ⑨ ⑩

MEALS

MEDICATIONS

Water Tracker 🍼 🍼 🍼 🍼 🍼 🍼 🍼

NOTES

....
....

DAY GOALS

1 ....
2 ....
3 ....

DATE
WEEK
LOCATION
WEIGHT

Mood Tracker 😕 😐 😖 😢 😠 😃

BEHAVIOR

INATTENTION

SHORT ATTENTION	① ② ③ ④ ⑤ ⑥ ⑦ ⑧ ⑨ ⑩
UNMOTIVATED / BORED	① ② ③ ④ ⑤ ⑥ ⑦ ⑧ ⑨ ⑩
SHORT ATTENTION	① ② ③ ④ ⑤ ⑥ ⑦ ⑧ ⑨ ⑩
FORGETFUL / CONFUSIONED	① ② ③ ④ ⑤ ⑥ ⑦ ⑧ ⑨ ⑩

HYPERACTIVITY

CONSTANTLY MOVING / TALKING	① ② ③ ④ ⑤ ⑥ ⑦ ⑧ ⑨ ⑩
STRUGGLING TO SIT STILL	① ② ③ ④ ⑤ ⑥ ⑦ ⑧ ⑨ ⑩
TOUCHING THINGS REPEATEDLY	① ② ③ ④ ⑤ ⑥ ⑦ ⑧ ⑨ ⑩
DIFFICULT SLEEPING	① ② ③ ④ ⑤ ⑥ ⑦ ⑧ ⑨ ⑩

IMPULSIVITY

ACTING WITHOUT THINKING	① ② ③ ④ ⑤ ⑥ ⑦ ⑧ ⑨ ⑩
INTERRUPTING OTHERS	① ② ③ ④ ⑤ ⑥ ⑦ ⑧ ⑨ ⑩
EASILY FRUSTRATED	① ② ③ ④ ⑤ ⑥ ⑦ ⑧ ⑨ ⑩
UNABLE TO HOLD BACK EMOTIONS	① ② ③ ④ ⑤ ⑥ ⑦ ⑧ ⑨ ⑩

MEALS

MEDICATIONS

Water Tracker 🍶 🍶 🍶 🍶 🍶 🍶 🍶

NOTES

....
....

DAY GOALS

1 ....
2 ....
3 ....

DATE

WEEK

LOCATION

WEIGHT

Mood Tracker 😟 😐 😖 😢 😠 😃

BEHAVIOR

INATTENTION

Behavior	Rating
SHORT ATTENTION	① ② ③ ④ ⑤ ⑥ ⑦ ⑧ ⑨ ⑩
UNMOTIVATED / BORED	① ② ③ ④ ⑤ ⑥ ⑦ ⑧ ⑨ ⑩
SHORT ATTENTION	① ② ③ ④ ⑤ ⑥ ⑦ ⑧ ⑨ ⑩
FORGETFUL / CONFUSIONED	① ② ③ ④ ⑤ ⑥ ⑦ ⑧ ⑨ ⑩

HYPERACTIVITY

Behavior	Rating
CONSTANTLY MOVING / TALKING	① ② ③ ④ ⑤ ⑥ ⑦ ⑧ ⑨ ⑩
STRUGGLING TO SIT STILL	① ② ③ ④ ⑤ ⑥ ⑦ ⑧ ⑨ ⑩
TOUCHING THINGS REPEATEDLY	① ② ③ ④ ⑤ ⑥ ⑦ ⑧ ⑨ ⑩
DIFFICULT SLEEPING	① ② ③ ④ ⑤ ⑥ ⑦ ⑧ ⑨ ⑩

IMPULSIVITY

Behavior	Rating
ACTING WITHOUT THINKING	① ② ③ ④ ⑤ ⑥ ⑦ ⑧ ⑨ ⑩
INTERRUPTING OTHERS	① ② ③ ④ ⑤ ⑥ ⑦ ⑧ ⑨ ⑩
EASILY FRUSTRATED	① ② ③ ④ ⑤ ⑥ ⑦ ⑧ ⑨ ⑩
UNABLE TO HOLD BACK EMOTIONS	① ② ③ ④ ⑤ ⑥ ⑦ ⑧ ⑨ ⑩

MEALS

MEDICATIONS

Water Tracker 🍼 🍼 🍼 🍼 🍼 🍼 🍼

NOTES

....
....

DAY GOALS		DATE	
1		WEEK	
2		LOCATION	
3		WEIGHT	

Mood Tracker 😟 😐 😖 😢 😠 😃

BEHAVIOR

INATTENTION

SHORT ATTENTION	① ② ③ ④ ⑤ ⑥ ⑦ ⑧ ⑨ ⑩
UNMOTIVATED / BORED	① ② ③ ④ ⑤ ⑥ ⑦ ⑧ ⑨ ⑩
SHORT ATTENTION	① ② ③ ④ ⑤ ⑥ ⑦ ⑧ ⑨ ⑩
FORGETFUL / CONFUSIONED	① ② ③ ④ ⑤ ⑥ ⑦ ⑧ ⑨ ⑩

HYPERACTIVITY

CONSTANTLY MOVING / TALKING	① ② ③ ④ ⑤ ⑥ ⑦ ⑧ ⑨ ⑩
STRUGGLING TO SIT STILL	① ② ③ ④ ⑤ ⑥ ⑦ ⑧ ⑨ ⑩
TOUCHING THINGS REPEATEDLY	① ② ③ ④ ⑤ ⑥ ⑦ ⑧ ⑨ ⑩
DIFFICULT SLEEPING	① ② ③ ④ ⑤ ⑥ ⑦ ⑧ ⑨ ⑩

IMPULSIVITY

ACTING WITHOUT THINKING	① ② ③ ④ ⑤ ⑥ ⑦ ⑧ ⑨ ⑩
INTERRUPTING OTHERS	① ② ③ ④ ⑤ ⑥ ⑦ ⑧ ⑨ ⑩
EASILY FRUSTRATED	① ② ③ ④ ⑤ ⑥ ⑦ ⑧ ⑨ ⑩
UNABLE TO HOLD BACK EMOTIONS	① ② ③ ④ ⑤ ⑥ ⑦ ⑧ ⑨ ⑩

MEALS	MEDICATIONS

Water Tracker 🍶 🍶 🍶 🍶 🍶 🍶 🍶

NOTES

....
....

DAY GOALS	
1	
2	
3	

DATE
WEEK
LOCATION
WEIGHT

Mood Tracker 😞 😐 😖 😢 😠 😃

BEHAVIOR

INATTENTION

SHORT ATTENTION	① ② ③ ④ ⑤ ⑥ ⑦ ⑧ ⑨ ⑩
UNMOTIVATED / BORED	① ② ③ ④ ⑤ ⑥ ⑦ ⑧ ⑨ ⑩
SHORT ATTENTION	① ② ③ ④ ⑤ ⑥ ⑦ ⑧ ⑨ ⑩
FORGETFUL / CONFUSIONED	① ② ③ ④ ⑤ ⑥ ⑦ ⑧ ⑨ ⑩

HYPERACTIVITY

CONSTANTLY MOVING / TALKING	① ② ③ ④ ⑤ ⑥ ⑦ ⑧ ⑨ ⑩
STRUGGLING TO SIT STILL	① ② ③ ④ ⑤ ⑥ ⑦ ⑧ ⑨ ⑩
TOUCHING THINGS REPEATEDLY	① ② ③ ④ ⑤ ⑥ ⑦ ⑧ ⑨ ⑩
DIFFICULT SLEEPING	① ② ③ ④ ⑤ ⑥ ⑦ ⑧ ⑨ ⑩

IMPULSIVITY

ACTING WITHOUT THINKING	① ② ③ ④ ⑤ ⑥ ⑦ ⑧ ⑨ ⑩
INTERRUPTING OTHERS	① ② ③ ④ ⑤ ⑥ ⑦ ⑧ ⑨ ⑩
EASILY FRUSTRATED	① ② ③ ④ ⑤ ⑥ ⑦ ⑧ ⑨ ⑩
UNABLE TO HOLD BACK EMOTIONS	① ② ③ ④ ⑤ ⑥ ⑦ ⑧ ⑨ ⑩

MEALS	MEDICATIONS

Water Tracker 🍼 🍼 🍼 🍼 🍼 🍼 🍼

NOTES

....
....

DAY GOALS

1 ....
2 ....
3 ....

DATE
WEEK
LOCATION
WEIGHT

Mood Tracker

BEHAVIOR

INATTENTION

Behavior	Rating
SHORT ATTENTION	1 2 3 4 5 6 7 8 9 10
UNMOTIVATED / BORED	1 2 3 4 5 6 7 8 9 10
SHORT ATTENTION	1 2 3 4 5 6 7 8 9 10
FORGETFUL / CONFUSIONED	1 2 3 4 5 6 7 8 9 10

HYPERACTIVITY

Behavior	Rating
CONSTANTLY MOVING / TALKING	1 2 3 4 5 6 7 8 9 10
STRUGGLING TO SIT STILL	1 2 3 4 5 6 7 8 9 10
TOUCHING THINGS REPEATEDLY	1 2 3 4 5 6 7 8 9 10
DIFFICULT SLEEPING	1 2 3 4 5 6 7 8 9 10

IMPULSIVITY

Behavior	Rating
ACTING WITHOUT THINKING	1 2 3 4 5 6 7 8 9 10
INTERRUPTING OTHERS	1 2 3 4 5 6 7 8 9 10
EASILY FRUSTRATED	1 2 3 4 5 6 7 8 9 10
UNABLE TO HOLD BACK EMOTIONS	1 2 3 4 5 6 7 8 9 10

MEALS

MEDICATIONS

Water Tracker

NOTES

....
....

www.ingramcontent.com/pod-product-compliance
Lightning Source LLC
LaVergne TN
LVHW011724060526
838200LV00051B/3020